Political and Social Change in the United States:

A Brief History, with the Articles of Confederation and Perpetual Union, the Declaration of Independence, the Constitution of the United States, and the Amendments to the Constitution

Edd Applegate

Political and Social Change in the United States:

A Brief History, with the Articles of Confederation and Perpetual Union, the Declaration of Independence, the Constitution of the United States, and the Amendments to the Constitution

Edd Applegate

Academica Press
Washington~London

Library of Congress Cataloging-in-Publication Data

Names: Applegate, Edd (author)
Title: Political and social change in the united states : a brief history, with the articles of confederation and perpetual union, the declaration of independence, the constitution of the united states, and the amendments to the constitution | Applegate, Edd
Description: Washington : Academica Press, 2021. | Includes references.
Identifiers: LCCN 2021943276 | ISBN 9781680539301 (hardcover) | 9781680539318 (paperback) | 9781680539554 (e-book)

Contents

Introduction

This book presents a brief history of the major political and social changes in the United States since the nation was founded. It includes the *Articles of Confederation and Perpetual Union*, the *Declaration of Independence*, the *Constitution of the United States*, and the *Amendments to the Constitution*. Considering these documents have contributed to the foundation on which the United States is based, all should be important to every living American. Every person old enough to vote should not only read these documents but thoroughly understand each.

During the presidency of Donald Trump, Democratic members of the House of Representatives impeached him—twice! Apparently, these members had not read the *Constitution of the United States*, the *Amendments to the Constitution*, and what the founders had said about impeachment (see *The Journal of the Constitutional Convention* by James Madison, the "Father of the Constitution" and the fourth president of the United States). If they had, more than likely some would have changed their votes. (By the way, no founder seriously thought any president would be impeached by the House of Representatives primarily because each believed the American people would elect an individual who not only understood but adhere to the documents on which the nation was founded. After all, many colonists had sacrificed their lives so that others could be free.)

Chapter 1

Political and Social Change in England from 1660 to 1775

The year 1660 marked a dramatic change in English history.

Termed the year of the Restoration because King Charles II returned from his exile of 17 years, 1660 marked the beginning of what was to become an important age. Between the mid-1600s and the late 1700s, England grew into a neo-classical empire that saw a great influx of immigrants, continued expeditions to other countries, including America and India, and the rise of Parliament as a powerful force in the English political structure. However, this neo-classical age came to an end when

> the coming of the industrial world due to industrial invention threw England into a revolution which brought in machinery and factories, changed the face of the landscape, expanded enormously the size of cities, and gave a profound shock to the existing habits of thought and outlook on life.[1]

Restored to the throne, Charles II was not without critics. Although many believed his reign would be an exceptional one, within a few years they saw that he was interested more in what the French had to offer primarily because his exile had been in France than in what his English subjects needed.

Charles II, a Catholic, resigned himself to his ministers' wishes and allowed them control of the government. As a result, the Church of England became more influential than Puritanism, which previously had been influential. After all, Oliver Cromwell, along with other Puritan leaders, had died.

Under Charles II, English citizens, particularly those living in London, experienced several major calamities that changed their lives. For instance, the bubonic plague killed thousands of citizens in 1665. The Great Fire of London, which immediately followed, destroyed thousands of buildings and killed thousands of citizens as well. A war with the Dutch Republic erupted in the mid-1660s, and an anti-Catholic rebellion occurred in the late 1670s. As if these were not grave enough, the King failed to produce an heir to the throne.

When Charles II died in 1685, his brother, James II, succeeded him as King and for three years flaunted his Catholicism. The Duke of Monmouth, who was Charles II's natural but illegitimate son, attempted to overthrow James II and was subsequently executed. Tensions between persons of different religions mounted until the King issued a *Declaration of Indulgence* which granted citizens of England the freedom of worship. Protestants had believed that the successor to the throne would be Mary, the King's daughter as well as an Anglican who had married William of Orange. When they realized that the King's new-born son, a baptized Catholic, might become King, they immediately rebelled. Consequently, James II lost his throne in 1688 to William and Mary.

Although William and Mary were welcomed to the throne, Parliament exercised its power, and William and Mary had to accept a *Bill of Rights*. No longer did a King or Queen have power because of his or her heredity. Rather, the power was granted by Parliament. However, the two-party system—Tories and Whigs (Cavaliers and Puritans), which had appeared during Cromwell's reign—failed to have an impact on English rule until after Mary's death in 1695 and William's death in 1702, when Mary's sister, Anne, became Queen.

During Anne's reign, a bitter struggle for power between the two parties erupted. Under the leadership of Robert Harley, Earl of Oxford, and Henry St. John, Viscount Bolingbroke, the Tories got control. When Anne died in 1714, the Whigs came to power and drove out the Tories.

When Anne died in 1714, Parliament demanded the next Queen or King be a Protestant. George, who became George I, King of the United Kingdom of Great Britain (England and Scotland had united under Anne's reign), was the only Protestant heir. George, who was the son of Sophia of Hanover, Germany, the granddaughter of James I, was not particularly interested in political affairs. Thus Parliament had a free hand. When George II succeeded his father to the throne in 1727, he, too, was disenchanted with English government. He was succeeded by his son, George III, in 1760, during the Seven Years' War (1756-1763) in which England successfully acquired Canada from France. George III tried to be a better King than his father and grandfather, but he failed to realize that England's colonial philosophy, which affected America, Canada, and India, was creating tensions abroad, especially in America.

* * *

During this period many English citizens contracted one or more diseases probably because of unsanitary conditions and the improper storage of food, not to mention rodents. Furthermore, personal hygiene was not a high priority. As if disease was not terrible enough, thieves, including highwaymen, robbed and even murdered citizens who tried to ride to town. Citizens who lived in London also experienced hardship and tragedy. For the most part, the thousands of buildings that burned in the Great Fire were inferior in construction and maintenance when compared to today's structures. Citizens, particularly those who lived in rural areas, since they seldom rode to town to hear the latest gossip, were illiterate and backward, socially speaking. Those who lived in London had to walk or ride on dirty streets. If they shopped at stores or visited coffee-houses, they did so during the day. During the night thieves and even murderers roamed the streets searching for victims.

Nonetheless, Britain prospered—first, from a large trade in the import and export of colonial produce; second, from a large trade in the export of agricultural produce such as grain; and third, from the Industrial Revolution. After the Great Fire, the citizenry eventually became enlightened from frequent visits to coffee-houses rebuilt of stone. Although problems such as war with another country plagued the Empire, the Empire survived. Even the internal bickering between Tory and Whig and Parliament and King could not destroy the nation or its people.

Notes:

1. George B. Woods, Homer A. Watt, George K. Anderson, and Earl J. Holzknecht, *The Literature of England: An Anthology and History* (Chicago: Scott, Foresman and Co., 1958), 812.

References:

Bright, J. Franck. *A History of England: Period III: Constitutional Monarchy: William and Mary to William IV: 1689-1837*. London: Longmans, Green, and Co., 1913.

Hoppit, Julian. *A Land of Liberty? England 1689-1727*. Oxford: Oxford University Press, 2000.

Jones, J. R. *Britain and the World, 1649-1845*. Brighton, Sussex: Havester Press, 1980.

Jones, J. R. *The Restored Monarchy, 1660-1688*. London: Macmillan, 1979.

Kearney, Hugh. *The British Isles: A History of Four Nations*. Cambridge: Cambridge University Press, 1995.

Morgan, Kenneth O., ed. *The Oxford Illustrated History of Britain*. Oxford: Oxford University Press, 2009.

Quinn, David Beers. *England and the Discovery of America: 1481-1620.* New York: Knopf, 1974.

Schama, Simon. *A History of Britain*. New York: Hyperion, 2000.

Chapter 2

Political and Social Change in the American Colonies from 1660 to 1783

Although James I of England was responsible for establishing his country's first colony—Virginia—in North America in 1607, Charles II furthered his country's interest in North America. Eventually, English colonies occupied the Atlantic coast from Canada to Florida. For instance, Pennsylvania was founded in 1681, and Philadelphia, which was founded a year later, became the greatest river port in the colonies. The Carolinas, which had been settled before Pennsylvania was founded, had numerous plantations that were developed by overseers and farmed by slaves from Africa.[1] The chartered colonies became Crown colonies, and governors appointed by the Crown replaced proprietors or managers. The influx of Puritans and Cavaliers increased the colonies' population,[2] and the American Indians were eventually stripped of their land.

The 13 English Colonies

Year Founded	Colony
1607	Virginia (Jamestown)
1620	Massachusetts (Plymouth and Massachusetts Bay Colony)
1626	New York (New Amsterdam, which was annexed by the English)
1633	Maryland
1636	Rhode Island
1636	Connecticut
1638	Delaware (New Sweden, which was annexed by the Dutch and then the English)
1638	New Hampshire
1653	North Carolina

1663	South Carolina
1664	New Jersey
1682	Pennsylvania
1732	Georgia

Other colonies such as Georgia were founded. However, the colonists were hemmed in by the French and the American Indians, and England, although it was the mother country, failed to help the colonists in their struggle to survive. Instead, laws were enacted to prohibit colonists from selling anything other than agricultural goods to England. Yet, colonists in the North caught fish, cut timber, hunted wildlife for furs, and even produced rum and beer, among other goods. Colonists in the South grew cotton, rice, sugar, and tobacco, among other crops. Concurrently, whenever something was purchased it had to come from England. Tariffs were placed on certain imports to keep the colonists from buying those products. Still, laws were passed to limit what could be produced such as iron.

According to colonists, one King or Queen was as evil as the next. Indeed, it made little difference whether James II, William and Mary, Anne, George I, George II, or George III reigned. The colonists' problems remained the same. Nonetheless, they had to be happy when England won the Seven Years' War or what is commonly called the French and Indian War in the American colonies. As a result of its victory against France, the British Empire got Canada, among other areas. Subsequently, colonists' fear of being invaded by France was eliminated.

However, as a result of England's debt because of the war, the Crown and Parliament restricted expansion as well as limited trade in North America. In addition, they passed various acts to raise revenue. For instance, the Stamp Act, which imposed a tax on all paper documents, was passed in 1765. Other acts, including the Townshend Acts, which taxed products imported to the colonies, followed. The colonists grew angry. They realized England was taxing them for revenue. Yet, as more than one patriot pointed out, they had no representation in Parliament. Eventually, several writers persuaded the colonists to unite and boycott goods from England.

In 1770, after English soldiers fired into a group of angry colonial protestors, killing five of them, Parliament repealed some of the legislation. However, other measures were enacted to serve the same purpose as the acts. Three years later Parliament passed the Tea Act, which was responsible for the rebellious Boston Tea Party. Subsequently, Parliament passed the Intolerable Acts. The colonists had had enough. Indeed, those living in Massachusetts armed themselves for combat.

Delegates from 12 colonies attended the First Continental Congress in Philadelphia in 1774 and pledged to defend Massachusetts. The Congress also made demands on England which the country ignored. When Governor Thomas Gage, who was also Commander-in-Chief of the British Army in America, was ordered to reestablish British rule, his military action was responsible for the War of Independence that started in 1775.

A year later, after much deliberation, the Continental Congress finally adopted the *Declaration of Independence,* which was written primarily by Thomas Jefferson and which explained the reasons for the colonies declaring their independence from England.[3] In 1777, the *Articles of Confederation and Perpetual Union* was written. Naming the new nation "The United States of America," the document gave Congress the authority to make treaties, maintain a military, and issue money. However, the central government could not levy taxes or regulate commerce. The *Articles of Confederation and Perpetual Union* was finally ratified in 1781 by the now established 13 states.

Finally, the War of Independence ended in 1783, when the states won their independence from England. Unfortunately, the central government faced many problems. Although the *Articles of Confederation and Perpetual Union* had been ratified, representatives of the states realized that a Constitution needed to be written and ratified.

* * *

Colonial society basically was rural and poor. Puritans as well as other colonists lived on farms. Few lived in cities, although cities grew rapidly because of the influx of people from other countries. If the farmer or plantation owner visited a city, he invariably traveled on roads made of mud. If he made his destination without loss of pocketbook or limb, he found streets made of cobblestones or gravel or, in some cases, dirt. As he walked by the shops he noticed silver buckles, delicate chinaware, exquisite fabrics, looking glasses, and other imported luxuries that were not sold in crossroads stores. If he stopped at a tavern, he drank beer or rum. Of course, if he had enough money and the desire, there were at least one or more women who were available for the evening.[4] The farmer or plantation owner more than likely returned home and warned his children about the city. As John M. Blum et al. wrote, "He seldom understood that the vice of the city, if not its prodigality, was mainly for transients like himself."[5]

Those who lived in cities were merchants who either purchased or traded produce, shipwrights who constructed ships, millers, instrument-makers, coopers, schoolmasters, barbers, craftsmen, and a host of others. City-dwellers had numerous problems that other Americans did not necessarily have. For instance, they had to deal with thieves and other criminals, unsanitary conditions, city traffic, closely built wooden houses and shops that frequently burned, and, of course, poverty whenever jobs were lost.

In order to tame a harsh wilderness, work had to be done, and the Puritans, among other groups, performed well. Although many were God-fearing people, they enjoyed the vices of man, including an occasional drink of alcohol and/or an occasional sexual affair. Still, the religious views of John Calvin dominated their lives. Predestination instilled in them a spark that ultimately ignited their will to achieve what man had not achieved before—freedom to grow strong both spiritually and economically.

Although witch hunts occurred in the 1690s, and differences between Puritan and Anglican and Quaker philosophies stirred fanatics to commit physical atrocities such as imprisonment or banishment before the 1700s, after 1720 religion experienced the Great Awakening. Revivals, which were more emotional perhaps than rational or intellectual, were held throughout the colonies for society's lower classes. From the Dutch Reformed churches of New Jersey to the Scotch-

Irish Presbyterian churches of Pennsylvania, revivalism, because it made religion more personal, prospered throughout the 1700s.

During this period, social, educational, and political institutions were founded. Colleges prepared students for the ministry, and enlightened them in philosophy, physics, and psychology. Literature, too, appeared. From histories and autobiographies, to plays and novels, colonists were provided literary entertainment. Perhaps the most important form of literature during this period was the advocating essay.

Notes:

1. It is estimated that several hundred thousand slaves were brought to the colonies in North America before they were freed in the 1800s.
2. Population in the colonies grew from about 2,000 in 1625 to more than 2,000,000 in 1775.
3. Thomas Jefferson had written a *Summary View of the Rights of British America: Set Forth in Some Resolutions Intended for the Inspection of the Present Delegates of the People of Virginia, Now in Convention* in 1774. Jefferson had argued that Great Britain had no rights to govern the colonies primarily because the colonies were independent of Britain. However, Jefferson was not the first colonist to present grievances or express independence. For instance, James Otis had written *Rights of the British Colonists Asserted and Proved* in 1764, in which he claimed Parliament could not tax the 13 colonies primarily because the colonies were not represented in Parliament. Stephen Hopkins had written *The Rights of Colonies Examined* the same year. Representatives from nine of the 13 colonies had stated their opposition to the Stamp Act in the *Declaration of Rights and Grievances*, which had been written primarily by John Dickinson in 1765. Richard Bland had written *An Inquiry into the Rights of the British Colonies* in 1766, in which he claimed that Parliament did not have the authority to tax any colony or enact legislation that interfered in any colony's affairs. Samuel Adams had written *A Statement of the Rights of the Colonies* in 1772, in which he claimed human rights came from God, not man. Adams claimed that government had the obligation to protect its citizens' lives, liberties, and property.

Of course, in addition to other political treatises, Jefferson was familiar with the *Magna Carta Libertatum*, which had been signed by King John of England in 1215, the *Mayflower Compact*, which had been signed by the leaders on board the *Mayflower* in 1620, and

England's *Bill of Rights* of 1689. In fact, such documents had influenced Jefferson's writing of the Preamble of the Constitution for Virginia as well as George Mason's writing of the *Declaration of Rights* for Virginia.

Jefferson undoubtedly had read Emerich de Vattel's *The Law of Nations: Or, Principles of the Law of Nations Applied to the Conduct and Affairs of Nations and Sovereigns*, which had been published in 1758, and especially John Locke's *Second Treatise on Government*, because of certain phrases that he expressed in the *Declaration of Independence*. Of course, Jefferson had read books by other philosophers. In short, he knew about the various governments, including those that had existed centuries before in Athens and in Rome. The reader should remember that learned individuals in Jefferson's time read newspapers, political treatises, and books. In fact, Jefferson, like other learned individuals at the time, had large libraries in their homes. Indeed, Jefferson owned several thousand books.

4. John M. Blum, Edmund S. Morgan, Willie Lee Rose, Arthur M. Schlesinger, Jr., Kenneth M. Stampp, and C. Vann Woodward, *The National Experience* (New York: Harcourt Brace Jovanovich, Inc., 1981), 64.

5. Blum, et al., 64.

References:

Adams, Willi P. *The First American Constitutions: Republican Ideology and the Making of the State Constitutions in the Revolutionary Era*. Chapel Hill: The University of North Carolina Press, 1980.

Andrews, Charles M. *The Colonial Period of American History*. New Haven: Yale University Press, 1964.

Berlin, Ira and Ronald Hoffman. *Slavery and Freedom in the Age of the American Revolution*. Charlottesville: University of Virginia Press, 1983.

Boorstin, Daniel J. *The Americans: The Colonial Experience*. New York: Random House, 1958.

Brant, Irving. *The Bill of Rights: Its Origin and Meaning*. Indianapolis: Bobbs-Merrill, 1965.

Bridenbaugh, Carl. *Cities in Revolt: Urban Life in America, 1743-1776*. New York: Alfred A. Knopf, 1968.

Bridenbaugh, Carl. *Cities in the Wilderness: The First Century of Urban Life in America*. New York: Oxford University Press, 1971.

Burns, James McGregor. *The American Experiment: The Vineyard of Liberty*. New York: Knopf, 1982.

Clark, Harry Hayden. *Thomas Paine: Representative Selections, with Introduction, Bibliography, and Notes*. New York: American Book Co., 1944.

Commager, Henry Steele. *The Empire of Reason: How Europe Imagined and America Realized the Englightenment*. New York: Doubleday/Anchor, 1977.

Davidson, Basil. *The African Slave Trade*. Boston: Little, Brown and Co., 1980.

Davidson, Philip. *Propaganda and the American Revolution, 1763-1783*. Chapel Hill: The University of North Carolina Press, 1941.

Draper, Theodore. *A Struggle for Power: The American Revolution*. New York: Times Books, 1996.

Ellis, Joseph J. *Founding Brothers: the Revolutionary Generation*. New York: Knopf, 2001.

Fast, Howard, ed. *The Selected Work of Tom Paine: Set in the Framework of His Life*. New York: Duell, Sloan and Pearce, 1945.

Ferling, John. *Setting the World Ablaze: Washington, Adams, Jefferson, and the American Revolution*. New York: Oxford University Press, 2000.

Flexner, James Thomas. *George Washington: the Forge of Experience, 1732-1775*. Boston: Little, Brown and Co., 1965.

Flexner, James Thomas. *George Washington in the American Revolution, 1775-1783*. Boston: Little, Brown and Co., 1967.

Haller, William. *Liberty and Reformation in the Puritan Revolution*. New York: Columbia University Press, 1967.

Haller, William. *The Rise of Puritanism*. New York: Columbia University Press, 1947.

Kettner, James H. *The Development of American Citizenship, 1608-1871*. Chaptel Hill: The University of North Carolina Press, 1978.

Klein, Herbert S. *The Middle Passage: Comparative Studies in the Atlantic Slave Trade*. Princeton, N.J.: Princeton University Press, 1978.

Kolchin, Peter. *American Slavery: 1619-1877*. New York: Hill & Wang, 1993.

Labaree, Leonard W. *Conservatism in Early American History*. Ithaca, N. Y.: Cornell University Press, 1972.

Langguth, A. J. *Patriots: The Men Who Started the American Revolution*. New York: Simon & Schuster, 1988.

Morison, Samuel E. *The Intellectual Life of Colonial New England*, 2nd ed. Westport, CT: Greenwood Press, 1980.

Morris, Richard B. *Government and Labor in Early America*. New York: Harper & Row, 1965.

Nash, Gary B. *Red, White, and Black: Peoples of Early North America*. Upper Saddle River, N.J.: Prentice-Hall, 1999.

Paine, Thomas. *Common Sense, The Rights of Man and Other Essential Writings*. New York: Meridian, 1984.

Parkman, Francis. *France and England in America* (2 vols.). New York: Library of America, 1983.

Rawley, James A. *The Transatlantic Slave Trade: A History*. New York: W. W. Norton, 1981.

Rossiter, Clinton, ed. *The Federalist Papers*. New York: Mentor, 1999.

Smith, Abbot E. *Colonists in Bondage: White Servitude and Convict Labor in America*. New York: W. W. Norton, 1971.

Street, William Warren. *Religion in Colonial America*. New York: Charles Scribner's Sons, 1953.

Wills, Gary. *Inventing America: Jefferson's Declaration of Independence*. Garden City, N.Y.: Doubleday, 1978.

Wright, Louis B. *The Cultural Life of the American Colonies, 1607-1763*. New York: Harper & Row, 1957.

Chapter 3

Political and Social Change in the United States from 1784 to 1900

After the War of Independence, representatives of the states reconvened to address the problems facing the new nation. George Washington, a former surveyor and general of the Continental Army who had led the new nation to victory, was a towering figure—both literally and figuratively. He presided at the Constitutional Convention in 1787.[1] He believed the *Articles of Confederation and Perpetual Union* were ineffective for a strong central government. Along with other patriots, he realized the country needed a constitution that united the states. When the *Constitution of the United States* was written primarily by James Madison and finally endorsed by the delegates and ratified by the states, Washington was pleased. After all, the document gave Congress the power it desperately needed. The new nation had a more binding document between its citizens and its central government—at least, on paper.

A new Congress was chosen. The electoral college unanimously elected George Washington the nation's first president in 1789. Washington did not believe in political parties and consequently did not belong to one. John Adams was his vice-president. Unlike modern presidents who exhibit partisanship when appointing individuals to cabinet positions, Washington appointed individuals who were intelligent and had different views to his cabinet. For instance, he appointed Alexander Hamilton and Thomas Jefferson who differed greatly, to say the least. Washington met with these individuals often.

Hamilton, who led what became the Federalist Party, believed in a strong central government and a sound monetary system. He favored legislation that benefited manufacturers and merchants. He also supported Great Britain.[2]

Jefferson was the leading spokesperson for the Anti-Federalists, which became known as the Democratic-Republicans. Jefferson opposed a strong central government because of its possible power over its citizens. States rights were important to him. He also did not think legislation favorable to industries and businesses should be passed. He supported the French.[3]

The first 10 Amendments to the constitution, which were called the "Bill of Rights," were written primarily by Madison to protect the rights of individuals. These 10 Amendments were ratified by most of the states in 1791. Although the *Constitution of the United States* applied to the federal government as well as every state, each state had its own constitution.

Still, the new nation struggled to form a democratic type of government. Indeed, lives had been lost during the Revolutionary War, and the country's economy was plagued by inflation and debt. The Revolutionary War had been costly.

As president, Washington realized the nation was in its infancy and needed a firm footing in order to survive. In short, it needed to grow and become prosperous. Members of Congress had realized this as well. For instance, in 1787 they had passed the Northwest Ordinance, an act that had encouraged people to purchase acreage inland. As a result, the federal government had received income from the sales. By 1790 the economy of the United States had improved.

In order to raise additional revenue, Congress passed the so-called Whiskey Tax in 1791. Farmers, particularly those in western Pennsylvania who used their excess grain to make distilled liquor, rebelled. Eventually, Washington had to lead troops into certain areas where farmers had opposed the tax. Although the troops crushed the rebellion, the federal government had a difficult time forcing the farmers to pay the tax.

Washington supported Hamilton's Bank of the United States, which Jefferson opposed, and his Tariff Act of 1792. Jefferson realized that Washington favored Hamilton's ideas regarding the country's financial situation over his. Consequently, it was not long before he resigned.

Although France claimed the United States was bound by the Franco-American Alliance of 1778 to support her in her war against England and other European countries, Washington issued a proclamation of neutrality because of monetary reasons and because England purchased most of the country's exports. Of course, France grew furious when Washington sent John Jay to London to negotiate, which resulted in Jay's Treaty of 1794. Although Washington's efforts were for the welfare of the nation, his action did not go unopposed. Indeed, Thomas Jefferson and other Democratic-Republicans disliked the treaty because of its favoritism. The country's press was divided over the issue.

Washington sent Thomas Pinckney to Madrid to negotiate another treaty for economic reasons. Pinckney's action resulted in the Treaty of San Lorenzo in 1795.

Washington oversaw the development of what would become Washington, D.C., before he left office. The capital city was located in an area donated by states. This area became the District of Columbia. (The District of Columbia was never to become a state.)

Without question, Washington had been an effective president. Furthermore, he set a precedent for presidents who followed him. In fact, if another founding father had been the first president, the nation may not have survived, considering how they differed in their views. Unfortunately, after he left office, the new nation saw political upheaval for 30 years.

Primarily because of the friction between the Federalist Party and the Democratic-Republicans, John Adams barely won the presidential election in 1796.

Adams had been educated at Harvard College. Like other patriots, he had been opposed to the oppressive acts imposed on the colonies by England. He had served as an influential member of the Continental Congress. In fact, in 1782, he had secured loans for the Revolutionary War and had helped negotiate peace with Great Britain.

As president, Adams tried to settle differences between the United States and France, but he was not successful. France declared war against the United States. As if this was not grave enough, the passage of the Alien and Sedition Acts in 1798 limited the freedom of the press primarily because publishers and others had been critical of the president and his administration. The acts also restricted the activities of those who had arrived from other countries.

Fortunately, the war with France, except for a few battles at sea, did not cause much harm to the United States. Eventually, France negotiated peace. Even though Adams had been victorious in a sense and saw his popularity increase, his break with Alexander Hamilton split the Federalist Party. In 1800, because of a tie in the electoral college, the election went to the House of Representatives. Thomas Jefferson won the presidency.

Jefferson had been educated at the College of William and Mary and had served as a member of the Continental Congress. His ideas had been expressed in the *Declaration of Independence*. He had served as secretary of state under President Washington. However, primarily because he had opposed Alexander Hamilton's ideas about a national bank and a strong central government, he had resigned in 1793.

Jefferson had led the Democratic-Republicans against Hamilton's Federalist Party. Although he had been defeated by John Adams for the presidency in 1796, he had served as Adams's vice-president.

Jefferson was the first president to take office in Washington, D.C. Unfortunately, the war against the pirates of the Barbary Coast as well as the Louisiana Purchase were costly to the nation. Nonetheless, the latter allowed the country to expand. Jefferson tried to obtain Florida, too, but he was not successful.

He won reelection in 1804, and approved several pieces of legislation, including the Embargo Act of 1807, which prohibited ships from sailing to foreign ports. Jefferson and his administration were criticized primarily because trade between the United States and European countries declined as a result. In 1809, a few days before he left office, Congress capitulated and passed the Non-Intercourse Acts.

James Madison had served as secretary of state under Jefferson before he was elected president in 1808. Educated at the College of New Jersey (now Princeton University), he had served as a member of the Continental Congress and had been responsible for the *Constitution of the United States* and the first 10 Amendments, which have become known as the "Bill of Rights."

Madison, like Jefferson, tried to protect the United States from getting involved in foreign matters. Because of his cabinet's hands-off attitude toward Great Britain and France, the country's relations with both degenerated. Madison attempted to gain respect from both nations, but relations grew exceedingly worse. Of course, what happened abroad had an impact on the United States. For instance, because France had owned parts of North America and because England had ruled the colonies, each country attempted to keep or recover what it had owned or controlled. However, because Great Britain had crushed France's military forces, she was convinced that she could pressure the United States—indeed, her ships had fired upon several ships that belonged to the United States Navy—into paying tariffs on overseas shipping. Madison closed the ports to shipping from overseas.

In 1812, after he won reelection, Madison and Congress declared war against Great Britain. The War of 1812 ended in 1815, when the Treaty of Ghent was signed. Although the war had occupied most of his administration's time, Madison approved the charter for a Second Bank of the United States before he left office.

James Monroe was elected president in 1816. Monroe had been educated at the College of William and Mary and had served in the military during the Revolutionary War. He had served as a United States Senator, a minister to France, a governor of Virginia, a minister to Great Britain, and a secretary of state under President Madison before he became president in 1817.

Monroe's administration was responsible for the Convention of 1818, which settled the northwest boundary between the United States and Great Britain. He signed the Missouri Compromise of 1820, which allowed Maine to enter the union as a free state and Missouri to enter the union as a slave state.

Monroe was reelected to a second term, and the nation continued to grow. In fact, by 1821, six states had been added to the union.

In 1823 Monroe spoke to Congress about prohibiting countries in Europe from establishing additional colonies in North and South America. Likewise, he believed the United States should promise that it would not exert itself in any country in Europe. This speech became known as the Monroe Doctrine.

John Quincy Adams was elected president in 1824. The oldest son of former President John Adams, John Quincy had been educated at Harvard College and had served as a minister to the Netherlands and to Prussia. Although he had been elected a United States Senator, he resigned in 1808 primarily because he opposed the Federalist Party's platform. He continued in politics, serving as the minister to Russia and, later, as secretary of state under President Monroe.

Adams had left the Federalist Party and had become a Democratic-Republican, like Henry Clay of Kentucky and Andrew Jackson of Tennessee, two senators who had run against him for the presidency. The election ended up in the House of Representatives of the United States. However, Clay encouraged members to support Adams, which they did, and Jackson lost.

Immediately, Adams asked Clay to serve as secretary of state. Of course, Jackson and his supporters criticized both, claiming they had made a deal.

As president, Adams supported the building of canals and roads and the exploration of the Northwest. Primarily because of the criticism he and his administration received, when he ran for reelection, he was defeated easily by Jackson.

During the 1820s and 1830s, public offices that had been appointive became elective. Voting increased as a result of fewer restrictions. An ideal democracy like no one had experienced materialized when Andrew Jackson's Democratic Party rivaled the revered Republican and later Whig parties.

Jackson, known as "Old Hickory," had captured the nation's attention when he led the United States Army against the British at the Battle of New Orleans in 1815. Later, he had fought the Seminole

Indians in the South. He had served in the House of Representatives of the United States and the United States Senate.

Primarily because of his legislative experience and military accomplishments on the battlefield, his popularity among the people increased. Although he ran for president against John Quincy Adams, the election had been decided in the House of Representatives. Adams had been selected. As mentioned, Jackson waged a vigorous campaign against Adams before Adams's first term ended and won. However, he and his wife, Rachel Robards, were criticized personally because of her divorce from her former husband, which apparently had been invalid. When her divorce had been final, she and Andrew married again, but the criticism would not cease. Rachel died soon after Jackson won the presidency, which caused Jackson to become bitter.

As president, Jackson surrounded himself with advisors who provided advice on politics and the economy, among other topics. These advisors made up the so-called "Kitchen Cabinet." He and his vice-president, John Caldwell Calhoun, disagreed about several issues, including nullification, which led to Calhoun's resignation.

Unfortunately, Jackson was responsible for forcing several Native American tribes from the southern states. These people had to give up their land and move west of the Mississippi River. As a result, not only did they lose their land, but many lost their lives as they journeyed west. This became known as "The Trail of Tears." This action was controversial, to say the least.

Still, Jackson's popularity remained high. In fact, he was reelected by a landslide.

Jackson opposed the Bank of the United States primarily because he did not necessarily believe the federal government should have such an institution. Consequently, when a bill for re-chartering the bank came to him, he vetoed it. Roger Brooke Taney, Jackson's secretary of the treasury, was instructed to use state banks instead. Jackson also opposed a high tariff, federal reapportionment of House seats, and distribution of land revenues to the states. He approved of westward and southward expansion, a strong foreign policy, and an independent treasury.

Jackson supported Martin Van Buren for president in 1836. Although Van Buren was elected, he faced several major problems. One was the financial crisis of 1837, which, reportedly, was caused by former President Jackson's policies.

Van Buren had served in the New York state senate and had been that state's attorney general before he had been elected to the United States Senate in 1821. Later, he had served as secretary of state and as vice-president under President Jackson.

Unfortunately, the financial crisis deepened in 1837. In fact, Congress passed a bankruptcy bill that allowed thousands of individuals to cancel their debts. Even several states repudiated their debts. Several state banks failed. The national debt increased. As if this was not grave enough, Van Buren was forced to try to fix a problematic banking system.

Van Buren thought the economy should be reformed. He called for an Independent Treasury System be established, which Congress finally approved before he ran for reelection in 1840. However, it was too little too late. He lost the election to William Henry Harrison. Apparently, people could not forget the financial crisis. They certainly could not forget Harrison's catchy slogan, "Tippecanoe and Tyler Too." Van Buren ran again for the presidency on the Free-Soil Party ticket in 1848, but he lost. However, he continued to be active in politics until he died in 1862.

William Henry Harrison had served in the United States Army and had defeated a Native American Indian attack at the Battle of Tippecanoe. Later, as a Whig, he had served in the House of Representatives of the United States and the United States Senate. He had waged an unsuccessful campaign against Martin Van Buren for the presidency in 1836. Four years later he ran again and won.

About a month after he took office, however, he contracted pneumonia and died. John Tyler, who served as his vice-president, succeeded him in 1841.

Tyler had been educated at the College of William and Mary and had served in the House of Representatives and the Senate of the United States before he had become vice-president and president.

As president, Tyler supported states' rights and opposed protective tariffs. He vetoed bills that would have reestablished the Bank of the United States. Like Harrison, Tyler was a Whig, but his views differed greatly from members of his cabinet. In fact, most eventually resigned.

Tyler also supported the expansion movement. He helped negotiate with Great Britain over the boundary between Maine and New Brunswick and he signed the Texas Act. However, primarily because of disagreements with other members of his party, Tyler did not have the necessary support to be reelected president.

James K. Polk was elected in 1844. Polk had been educated at the University of North Carolina and had practiced law in Tennessee before he entered politics. A Democrat, he had served in the House of Representatives of the United States and as governor of Tennessee.

As president, he believed in expanding the nation all the way to the Pacific Ocean. This westward expansion became known as Manifest Destiny, which was written about by more than one journalist who favored people settling the land in the West. Polk signed a treaty with Great Britain that settled the dispute regarding the Northwest Territory. He eventually secured the southwest territory, which had been part of Mexico.

Some Americans who inhabited the Republic of Texas had slaves. At the time, Texas was under the Mexican government which prohibited slavery. The issue, perhaps more than any other, led to revolution. When the United States attempted to annex Texas in 1845, Mexico declared war. Many newspapers supported the war, but there were some that did not. For instance, Horace Greeley protested against it in the *New York Tribune*. Frederick Douglass, a former slave who published the *North Star* in Rochester, New York, criticized it as well. Of course, these journalists, like other thinking people, realized that more land acquired would be argued over by those from the North as well as by those from the South. In short, they wondered if the states from this land would enter the Union as free or as slave states.

Within three years Mexico was defeated. The Treaty of Guadalupe Hidalgo, which officially ended the war, was signed. As a result, Mexico sold Texas, northern California, and New Mexico to the United States.

Polk was also interested in fiscal reform. For instance, he reduced tariffs, which was opposed by manufacturers and merchants in the United States. He supported the Independent Treasury System that former President Van Buren had started but the Whigs had abolished.

Although he accomplished what he had intended, he did not seek reelection.

Zachary Taylor had grown up on a farm in Kentucky and had spent years in the United States Army. As an officer, he had fought during the War of 1812. He had experienced other wars, too, including the Mexican War. Indeed, Taylor had been victorious in battle after battle. Newspaper reporters had covered his heroic engagements, and the Whigs realized they had a presidential candidate in the making.

When Polk decided not to seek reelection, Taylor ran for the presidency in 1848. A Whig, Taylor defeated Lewis Cass, a Democrat, and Van Buren, who had become a Free Soiler. As president, Taylor signed the Clayton-Bulwer Treaty with Great Britain. Unfortunately, he became ill and died in 1850. He had served as president a little over a year.

His vice-president, Millard Fillmore, became president.

Fillmore had practiced law in Buffalo, New York, before he had been elected to the House of Representatives of the United States in 1832. A Whig, he had helped establish a low-rate tariff in 1842.

As president, Fillmore appointed Daniel Webster as secretary of state. Webster and Henry Clay of Kentucky argued for what became known as the Compromising Measures of 1850. These measures contained several concessions, including a new Fugitive Slave Law, which allowed the federal government to help slave owners in the South recover any escaped slaves. To say the least, this law, perhaps more than any other of the measures, was criticized because it caused fear among African-Americans who had found freedom in the North through the Underground Railroad, which had been organized by various individuals, including ministers, for the purpose of helping slaves. In addition,

California entered the Union as a free state, which caused southerners to react negatively.

As a result of these measures passing, the Whigs chose General Winfield Scott over Fillmore for the election in 1852. However, Franklin Pierce, a Democrat, defeated Scott.

Pierce had been educated at Bowdoin College before he had entered politics. He had served in the House of Representatives and later the Senate of the United States. He had even served as a high-ranking officer in the Mexican War.

As president, Pierce was indecisive, to say the least. Slavery was becoming a major issue in the United States, particularly in the North where the practice was frowned upon by politicians, professional people, and newspaper publishers and editors. Of course, other problems such as the various movements that occurred shaped public opinion, and sectional loyalty which prejudiced members of certain groups or areas of the country did not help the situation. When Stephen A. Douglas's Kansas-Nebraska Act, which allowed slavery in territory that had been reserved for free states, appeared in 1854, Pierce supported it. The bill basically repealed the Missouri Compromise to benefit railroads, which were interested in westward expansion. However, the people who moved to the Kansas Territory were divided over the issue of slavery. In fact, this territory became known as Bloody Kansas as fight after fight broke out. Unfortunately, Pierce did not know how to resolve the dispute.

Northerners who were against slavery reacted negatively to the bill and created the new Republican Party.

Pierce also supported expansion, including the idea of purchasing Cuba from Spain or taking it by military action. However, he disliked the Clayton-Bulwer Treaty, which had given Great Britain an equal interest in any isthmian canal that might be built in Central America.

Primarily because of his support of the Kansas-Nebraska Act, Pierce was not re-nominated for president in 1856. Instead, John C. Freemont became the candidate of the new Republican Party, but he lost to James Buchanan, a Democrat.

Buchanan had been educated at Dickinson College in his home state of Pennsylvania. In 1821 he had been elected to the House of

Representatives of the United States. Formerly a member of the Federalist Party, he had become a Democratic-Republican and had supported Andrew Jackson for president. Later, he had been elected to the United States Senate and had served as secretary of state under President James K. Polk and as a minister to Great Britain under President Franklin Pierce.

As president, Buchanan asked Congress to purchase Cuba from Spain, but the Republicans stood in the way. When Minnesota entered the Union as a free state in 1858, the South's attitudes toward the North worsened as a result.

Buchanan heard numerous cries for the southern states to secede from the Union. Slavery, he realized, was important to the South, even though most people who lived in the South did not own slaves. In fact, most people who lived in the South were poor. Buchanan thought the issue of slavery would be handled by the United States Supreme Court. In 1857 the Supreme Court heard the Dred Scott v Sandford case. Scott, a slave, had been owned by Dr. John Emerson who had died in 1846. Since Scott had lived with Dr. Emerson in states and territories that had been free, he thought he should be free because Dr. Emerson had died. Unfortunately, Chief Justice Roger Taney ruled that Scott was a slave and was the property of his owner. Of course, landowners in the South appreciated the ruling, but the Democrats, particularly those in the North, were not happy.

In 1859, when a dispute erupted over Kansas being admitted to the Union, Buchanan tried to appease the South by encouraging members of Congress to allow Kansas in as a slave state. Although he was determined to preserve the Union, he failed to take effective action. Several southern states seceded. Of course, his inaction caused many members of his party to criticize him and not support him for reelection.

Abraham Lincoln, a Republican, was elected president in 1860.

Lincoln had been born in a log cabin in Kentucky. His mother had died when he was young. His father had remarried and had moved the family to Indiana and then to Illinois. Except for the alphabet and basic arithmetic, Lincoln had little education. Yet, he had learned to read well enough to study law. In fact, he had passed the bar in 1836.

Lincoln had moved to Springfield, Illinois, and had practiced law. Later, he had served in the state legislature. Ann Rutledge, the woman he had loved, had died of typhoid fever. Eventually, in 1842, Lincoln had married Mary Todd of Kentucky. However, they were extremely different. Indeed, he had come from a poor family. She had come from a wealthy one. He had been disorderly most of his life. She had been the opposite. He seldom had worried about his appearance. She had—and often. He had a sense of humor and had often told funny stories. She had not.

Lincoln had realized that Mary was different. He also had realized that he may not have been president if she had not encouraged him to pursue the position.

Lincoln had served one term in the House of Representatives of the United States primarily because he had opposed the Mexican War, which had irritated the voters in Illinois. After he had lost, he had continued practicing law. In 1855 he had campaigned for the United States Senate, but had lost. Apparently, the voters had not forgotten.

In 1858 he had debated Senator Stephen A. Douglas, a Democrat, about slavery. Douglas had been a successful politician. He had much to lose, but Lincoln had little to lose. One of the most impressive speeches given during these debates had been "A House Divided" by Lincoln.

> "A house divided against itself cannot stand."
>
> I believe this government cannot endure permanently half *slave* and *half* free.
>
> I do expect the Union to be *dissolved*—I do not expect the house to *fall*—but I *do* expect it will cease to be divided.
>
> It will become *all* one thing or *all* the other.
>
> Either the *opponents* of slavery, will arrest the further spread of it, and place it where the public mind shall rest in the belief that it is in the course of ultimate extinction; or its *advocates* will push it forward till it shall become alike awful

> in *all* the States, *old* as well as *new*, *North* as well as *South*.[4]

The debates had been covered by the press. As a result, Lincoln's stature had grown while Douglas's stature had not.

When Lincoln won the presidency in 1860, he watched several states in the South form the Confederate States of America. Since Buchanan was still president, Lincoln could not take action.

On Inauguration Day, he argued against secession but assured the South that he would not interfere wherever slavery existed. As president, however, he intended to apply federal laws to all the states. Unfortunately, the Confederates fired on supply ships sailing to Ft. Sumter, an act that started the American Civil War. Lincoln was dismayed, but he had to save the Union, which now consisted of 20 states. There were 11 Confederate states. Delaware, Kentucky, Maryland, Missouri, and West Virginia were considered Border States.

States of the Union during the Civil War

California	Nevada
Connecticut	New Hampshire
Illinois	New Jersey
Indiana	New York
Iowa	Ohio
Kansas	Oregon
Maine	Pennsylvania
Massachusetts	Rhode Island
Michigan	Vermont
Minnesota	Wisconsin

Confederate States during the Civil War

Alabama	North Carolina
Arkansas	South Carolina
Florida	Tennessee
Georgia	Texas
Louisiana	Virginia
Mississippi	

The Union had advantages over the Confederate states. For instance, there were twice as many inhabitants, more manufacturing firms, and more railroads. However, Lincoln had to find capable officers to train volunteers. In addition, he needed an efficient navy that could blockade the South. His efforts in recruiting men increased the size of the Union Army, but the jealousies between high-ranking officers were evident. Initially, the Union Army lost several strategic battles, which caused morale problems among the officers and their soldiers. Even civilians in the North complained about the war.

In 1861, in order to pay for the war, Congress passed the first bill concerning an income tax. About a year later the Battle of Shiloh occurred in Tennessee, near the Mississippi border. Thousands of Union and Confederate soldiers were wounded or killed in one of the bloodiest battles of the war.

General George B. McClellan complained about not having enough artillery, men, or supplies. He was hesitant to engage the enemy. Eventually, he and his troops engaged the enemy at Antietam. The outcome was more positive than negative for the North, but Lincoln thought McClellan could have shortened the war if he had been more aggressive whenever and wherever he engaged the enemy. Consequently, Lincoln replaced McClellan as the leader of the Union Army. In fact, he tried other generals before he found General Ulysses S. Grant.

In 1862 Lincoln signed the Morrill Land Grant Act, which provided public lands to states to sell. Income from the sales had to be applied to building colleges that offered agriculture and mechanic arts or be given to colleges to develop such programs. The same year emancipation of the slaves became an official federal issue, when President Lincoln issued his Emancipation Proclamation, which was finally issued on January 1, 1863. Although Congress failed to enact it until after the war, the document, perhaps more than any other at the time, was important to the Union. After all, it provided a purpose for the war.

In 1863 the Union experienced victories at Vicksburg, Mississippi, and at Gettysburg, Pennsylvania. Now, General Ulysses S. Grant was in charge of the Union Army. However, Gettysburg was another bloody battle in which thousands of soldiers were wounded or killed. Lincoln spoke at the dedication of the cemetery at Gettysburg, November 19, 1863. The following is part of his address:

> Four score and seven years ago our fathers brought forth on this continent, a new nation, conceived in Liberty, and dedicated to the proposition that all men are created equal.
>
> Now we are engaged in a great civil war, testing whether that nation, or any nation so conceived and so dedicated, can long endure. We are met on a great battle-field of that war. We have come to dedicate a portion of that field, as a final resting place for those who here gave their lives that that nation might live. It is altogether fitting and proper that we should do this.[5]

Although Lincoln's popularity increased after General William T. Sherman and his troops took Atlanta in 1864, his administration suffered severe criticism. However, Jefferson Davis's Confederate administration suffered severe criticism as well. Indeed, certain leaders in the southern states realized that slavery had to be abolished in order for the South to survive. Southerners living in the North, on the other hand, cared little about emancipation of the slaves.

Like the South, the North experienced heavy casualties in 1864. General McClellan, who had become the Democratic candidate for president, claimed the war was a failure and that the North should negotiate peace. However, Lincoln and his vice-president, Andrew Johnson, won the election.

In 1865 General Robert E. Lee surrendered to General Grant at Appomattox Court House in Virginia. Finally, the war was over. Lincoln had to consider Reconstruction. Although the Senate of the United States had passed the Thirteenth Amendment, which outlawed slavery, a year earlier, the House of Representatives had not. Of course, Lincoln asked the House to reconsider it, which it did.

Unfortunately, Lincoln did not live to execute his Reconstruction program because he was assassinated in early 1865. John Wilkes Booth, an actor who strongly supported the South, shot Lincoln as he watched a play at Ford's Theater in Washington, D. C.

Andrew Johnson had been born in North Carolina but had moved to Tennessee in 1826. He had served in the House of Representatives and later in the Senate of the United States. He had believed strongly in the Homestead Act and had thought that emancipation should be decided by the states. Although a Jacksonian Democrat from the South, he had been elected vice-president and had served under President Lincoln, a Republican.

When Lincoln was assassinated, Johnson became president. He attempted to restore the Union to normalcy, but several so-called Radical Republicans in the House of Representatives and the Senate of the United States strongly opposed him. Indeed, they thought the South should be severely punished.

Nonetheless, he implemented his Reconstruction program, which called for the pardoning of Confederates and repudiate their debts. He appointed temporary governors of the southern states. He stipulated that each state had to abolish slavery, ratify the Thirteenth Amendment, and have allegiance to the Union, among other demands.

Eventually, so-called Black Codes, which varied from state to state in the South, were written to control African-Americans who had been freed. Once word about such legislation reached Washington, problems between the Republicans in Congress and the president developed. In short, they differed greatly.

The Freedmen's Bureau, which had been established for the purpose of helping former slaves, had failed to encourage African-Americans to improve their lives. When Congress passed a law that would extend the bureau, Johnson vetoed it. When Congress passed a basic Civil Rights bill that would have ended the Black Codes, Johnson vetoed it as well. However, Congress overrode his veto.

In 1867 Republicans in the Congress passed several Reconstruction acts primarily because they thought President Johnson's Reconstruction program had by-passed Congress. Although Johnson vetoed the bills, the Republicans overrode his veto. Their acts called for regions being governed by military officers in the South. States had to draft constitutions that allowed African-Americans the right to vote.

Each state had to accept the Fourteenth Amendment, which provided citizenship to former slaves.

Although Johnson vetoed these acts, the Republicans overrode his veto. Then he tried to veto the newly passed Tenure of Office Act primarily because it dissuaded a president from removing any official who had been confirmed by the United States Senate, which he thought was unconstitutional. His veto was overridden. When Johnson attempted to dismiss Secretary of War Edwin M. Stanton, who had been appointed by former President Lincoln and who had been confirmed by the Senate, articles of impeachment were brought against him. At the trial in the Senate, he was acquitted by a narrow margin.

Johnson's presidency, however, was over. He had confronted the Radical Republicans in Congress once too often. Indeed, they had fought him at every turn—and had won.

Johnson left Washington after his presidency. In 1875, after he was elected to the United States Senate, he returned. Unfortunately, he died a few months later.

In 1868 Ulysses S. Grant, a Republican, was elected president. Grant had been the general who had been responsible for the North winning the war. Grant had been born in Ohio and had graduated from the United States Military Academy at West Point, New York. He had served in the Mexican War and, later, had left the military and had worked at several jobs.

Grant had obtained a commission as an officer after the Civil War had started. In 1861 he had been promoted to a general and had led men into battles in various southern states. Primarily because of his success on the battlefield, Lincoln had awarded him command of the Union Army. In April 1865, he had accepted General Robert E. Lee's surrender at Appomattox Court House in Virginia. Grant had become a heroic figure.

As president, Grant never questioned the Radical Republicans who served in Congress about their policies regarding Reconstruction. In 1870 he helped create the Department of Justice, which prosecuted the Ku Klux Klan (KKK). The Klan had been founded by southern whites primarily to instill fear in African-Americans. Using intimidation and acts of violence, members of the organization had broken several laws. In 1871 he helped create the first Civil Service Commission.

Unfortunately, several leaders in his administration were connected to unscrupulous businessmen who enjoyed earning money by not having to work honestly for it. As a result, many other Republicans and Democrats were offended by certain members of his administration. In short, they questioned these members' ethics, to say the least. Consequently, they supported Horace Greeley, a prominent journalist who had criticized the war, for president.

Grant won reelection, but his second term faced more problems. Grant continued to appoint people he agreed with or who supported him, even if it had been determined that some had been involved in illegal activities. Without question, he stood by his friends, but some caused his presidency to be severely criticized. For instance, Grant's vice-president, Schuyler Colfax, had benefited from the Credit Mobilier of America affair, which involved a construction company that had charged the Union Pacific Railroad outlandish fees. Grant's secretary of war, W. W. Belknap, was forced to resign because he had taken bribes. His secretary of the treasury, W. W. Richardson, was implicated in an illegal scheme that had earned him money. Of course, there were others, including his private secretary, Orville Babcock. However, Grant was never implicated in any crime.

In 1873 people learned about the corruption. Consequently, the publicity, not to mention the economic depression at the time, damaged the Republican Party. In fact, in 1874 many Republicans running for Congress were defeated. However, the Republican candidate for president, Rutherford B. Hayes, was not because of a special electoral commission and the United States Senate.

Grant retired from politics and, later, wrote the *Personal Memoirs of Ulysses S. Grant* shortly before his death. When published, his well-written memoirs were purchased by thousands of readers who were interested in learning about his life.

Rutherford B. Hayes had been born in Ohio and had attended Kenyon College and the Harvard Law School. He had practiced law in

Cincinnati and had served in the House of Representatives of the United States before he had served as governor of Ohio.

Nominated for president in 1876, Hayes received fewer popular and electoral votes than Governor Samuel J. Tilden, a Democrat of New York. Tilden had been responsible for breaking the Boss Tweed Ring at Tammany Hall. However, the Republicans disputed the electoral returns in several southern states and demanded these returns be scrutinized by a special electoral commission. The commission and the United States Senate awarded the electoral votes to Hayes, which caused problems for his presidency. For instance, many in Congress, particularly those in the House of Representatives, believed he had no right to be president.

Still, as president, Hayes withdrew the military from the South and tried to restore its economy by providing federal subsidies. In addition, he tried to implement federal measures that would make elections in the South open to African-Americans as well as whites. However, he was pressured into withdrawing the measures. Subsequently, African-Americans were eliminated from voter registrations. Southern states enacted laws that required African-Americans to be able to read and write in order to vote. Consequently, African-Americans became segregated.

Hayes favored change in the civil service, and opposed policies that he thought would worsen the economic depression of the 1870s. He informed members of his party and the public that he was not interested in seeking another term. When his presidency ended, he returned to Ohio.

James A. Garfield, another Republican, became president in 1880. Chester A. Arthur was his vice-president.

Garfield had been born in a cabin in Ohio and had worked his way through Williams College. He had been a teacher and preacher before he had served as a high-ranking officer in the Civil War. He had experienced action at Shiloh and Chickamauga. In 1863 he had been elected to the House of Representatives of the United States and had strongly supported the administration of President Lincoln.

Although Garfield faced several problems, including the Post Office Department and the civil service, he was shot by Charles Guiteau, a disgruntled office-seeker, in 1881. Garfield died several weeks later.

Chester A. Arthur became president.

Arthur had been born in Vermont and had attended Union College in New York. He had practiced law in New York City and in 1871 had been appointed collector of customs for the Port of New York. Arthur had been responsible for more than 1,000 jobs. However, when former President Hayes had tried to rid what was called the "spoils system," which had been nothing more than political patronage that had led to unethical behavior and even crime, Arthur had been removed from his job.

As president, Arthur strongly opposed corruption in government, no matter where it existed. Consequently, he advocated for the Civil Service Reform Act—better know as the Pendleton Act—to be passed by Congress, which it did in 1883. This act established a Civil Service Commission that administered examinations to both prospective employees and current employees of the federal government.

Although Arthur supported tariff acts that protected manufacturers and merchants, the Republicans nominated former secretary of state, James G. Blaine, for president in 1884, but Grover Cleveland was elected president.

Arthur left the presidency and died in 1886.

Grover Cleveland had been born in New Jersey and had practiced law in Buffalo, New York. He had served as governor of the state in the 1880s. An honest and independent thinker, Cleveland had been strong on law and order.

Cleveland caused members of the Democratic Party to rejoice. Indeed, he was the first Democrat to be elected president in more than 20 years. However, Cleveland faced a divided Congress. Unlike most Democrats, he was conservative when it came to political policies. For instance, he opposed barriers to competition. He opposed pensions to war veterans. He made certain that any western land that had been obtained by fraudulent means was restored to the public domain. He believed in the separation of the three branches of the federal government. For instance, he did not allow himself to be influenced by any member of Congress and he did not attempt to manipulate any member, either. He believed in the veto and was not afraid to use it.

In 1887 the Interstate Commerce Act was enacted to legislate corruptible practices employed primarily by railroads. The same year the cattle industry was severely curtailed by a blizzard. Cleveland spoke against high protective tariffs, which more than likely caused him to lose reelection in 1888.

Benjamin Harrison, a Republican, became president.

Harrison, the grandson of William H. Harrison, had been born in Ohio and had graduated from Miami University in Ohio. He had practiced law in Indianapolis, Indiana, and had become a prominent member of the Republican Party. He had served as an officer in the Union Army and had been elected to the United States Senate.

As president, Harrison supported protective tariffs, including the McKinley Tariff Act of 1890. This act was designed to help farmers by protecting agricultural products, but it actually increased tariff schedules that caused higher prices on agricultural products. Instead of helping farmers the measures only ignited Farmers' Alliances which engaged in politics. He supported the Sherman Antitrust Act of 1890, which stipulated that monopolies that restrained trade between states or foreign countries were illegal. However, this act was not used to break up any industrial monopoly until 10 years later. He also supported the Sherman Silver Purchase Act of 1890, which forced the federal government to buy silver that was mined in the West.

Primarily because Harrison had supported the McKinley Tariff Act, which had caused higher prices, he was defeated by Grover Cleveland in 1892.

In his second term as president, Cleveland faced an economic depression that lasted several years. Farming was paralyzed and industries suffered. Cleveland encouraged Congress to repeal the Sherman Silver Purchase Act in 1893. However, in 1894, Congress passed the Wilson-Groman Tariff Act, which Cleveland opposed and consequently vetoed, but Congress overrode his veto. The same year he had to send the military to Chicago to crush the Pullman Strike, which irritated several members of his party.

Probably because of Cleveland's position toward the workers in Chicago, the Democrats nominated William Jennings Bryan for president in 1896. However, Bryan was defeated by William McKinley, a Republican.

McKinley had been born in Ohio and had attended Allegheny College in Pennsylvania. He had served in the Civil War and, later, had practiced law in Ohio. In 1876 he had been elected to the House of Representatives of the United States. He had supported the so-called McKinley Tariff Act of 1890. He had served as governor of Ohio before he had been nominated for president in 1896.

As president, McKinley's administration faced possible war with Spain over Cuba, where many Cubans had begged the United States for support. These Cubans claimed they had been oppressed or ignored by Spain and wanted their freedom.

In 1896, when the battleship *Maine* blew up in Havana harbor, William Randolph Hearst's *New York Journal* and Joseph Pulitzer's *New York World* blamed Spain. The Congress and President McKinley declared war on Spain.

The war was fought primarily at sea, although Theodore Roosevelt and his Rough Riders stormed San Juan Hill. Within weeks, the war was over. Spain had been defeated. In December, Spain gave Cuba its independence. The United States received Guam, the Philippines, and Puerto Rico in exchange for several million dollars.

Congress passed the Dingley Tariff Act in 1896, and McKinley signed it. The act increased duties on imports in 1897. The amount of gold increased and the Gold Standard Act, which was enacted in 1900, required the Treasury of the United States to maintain a minimum gold reserve. Before 1900 prosperity returned to the farmer and the industrialist. Financial support for industrial expansion was available from such financiers as J. P. Morgan.

* * *

During the 1800s, even though the country experienced numerous societal differences and a major civil war, the United States progressed. In fact, some would say the nation progressed at a rapid pace. Commerce gave rise to regional specialization and contributed to the growth of cities.

By 1860 the nation had prospered to the extent that it no longer depended on Europe to purchase its goods. The West opened up. Innovations in technology helped increase production, particularly in textiles. Because of exploitation industrial workers formed unions. Banks increased in number. Commerce became complex. Transportation projects such as canals, railroads, and turnpikes advanced and helped reduce costs of certain products. Even steamboats on rivers contributed. According to George Rogers Taylor, the rapid development of a national transportation system made interregional trade economically feasible.[6] In the South cotton became the chief asset. In the North factories supported employees who lived in cities. For most of the nation's citizenry agriculture was the primary means of livelihood.

Immigrants from the Old World, including England, Ireland, and Germany, arrived daily. Immigrants from Germany fared well, while those from Ireland fared poorly. Germans, who had money or access to financial aid, purchased farms. The Irish, for the most part, congregated in cities, where they worked at low-paying jobs. Usually, because of their low wages, they had to live in slums filled with pestilence and disease. African-Americans, even those who lived in the North, were worse off, for they had to take jobs that whites refused. In addition, many faced hostility from whites. Freedom for many of them was merely a word.

City government, in order to survive and expand its obligations to the citizenry, was forced to tax. Police forces came into existence, garbage was removed, streets were improved, and education progressed.

Religion, similar to what was happening in Europe, witnessed a rise in interdenominational revivalism before 1840. City after city received scores of ministers who believed that cities were the dens where Satan dwelled.

As the country progressed, so did its citizenry. Wealth was obtained by a select few, however. For instance, throughout the latter 1800s the South suffered. In fact, in the South many whites were almost as poor as African-Americans. In fact, the southern states ranked the lowest in every statistical index at the time.

Various movements, on the other hand, affected more people. These movements, which swept across the country, were created by specific groups for certain issues, such as women's rights, capital punishment, workers' rights, education, mental health, temperance, and pacifism. Abolitionism was the most controversial. Other movements, which included Communistic communities such as Brook Farm, were not as popular as their promoters hoped.

The nation's population increased, and when nine million immigrants entered the nation in the late 1800s, citizens of the United States grew concerned. The western territory was settled and eventually gained statehood. Silver as well as gold was discovered. Cattle became an industry not only in Texas but in the Dakotas. Railroads branched from the East and the West, and in 1869 one complete line crossed the American landscape. Unfortunately, owners of railroads realized their power; consequently, they fixed prices, they monopolized transportation, they discriminated against certain customers, and they used their power to influence local and state legislators and subsequent legislation.

The Native American was pushed aside until federal legislation intervened.

Industry, which had grown from the beginning of the century, more than doubled in production between the late 1870s and the 1890s. Production of iron and steel in the United States, unlike the rest of the world, increased. Among other inventions, the telephone, phonograph, electric light bulb, and typewriter spawned new industries. Petroleum used for engines as well as heating and lighting created another major industry.

J. P. Morgan, Sr., helped the federal government financially in the late 1800s. In exchange for gold, he received federal bonds, which he sold at a profit. However, Morgan was not alone in accumulating vast wealth during this period. Andrew Carnegie, a steel magnate, was another. Both men were interested in seeing certain railroads cross the country. Of course, as mentioned, others were interested, too, including several members of Congress as well as President Grant's Vice-President

Schuyler Colfax and Vice-President Henry Wilson, both of whom had earned money from the company, Credit Mobilier of America, which had been awarded construction contracts for the Union Pacific Railroad.

In addition to Morgan and Carnegie, there were other extremely wealthy individuals, including Cornelius Vanderbilt, Jay Gould, John D. Rockefeller, and several others. These individuals owned industries and eventual trusts, which were monopolies. Company mergers also appeared. Of course, tensions between management and employees ensued. Subsequently, laborers formed more unions, a few of which became national in size. Through strikes and boycotts labor tried to obtain higher wages, better working conditions, and fewer hours. However, before the turn of the century, because of several incidents in which people were either injured or killed, labor unions received severe criticism from the press and the public.

Notes:

1. The Constitutional Convention consisted of 55 delegates who met in what is called Independence Hall in Philadelphia. These delegates were well-read. In fact, almost half had graduated from college. Many were lawyers. Many had served in the Revolutionary War. Contrary to popular belief, fewer than half actually owned slaves. Of course, a few, such as George Washington and Thomas Jefferson, owned numerous slaves primarily because they owned large farms.
2. Alexander Hamilton had been educated at King's College (now Columbia University) and had served in the Continental Army during the Revolutionary War. He was one of the major essayists of the *Federalist Papers*. He argued for the ratification of the *Constitution of the United States*. Along with other Federalists such as James Madison and John Jay, Hamilton believed in a strong central government.
3. Thomas Jefferson, like Patrick Henry, George Mason, Samuel Adams, John Hancock, James Monroe, George Clinton, Robert Yates, and Richard Henry Lee, among others, was an Anti-Federalist. These individuals objected to the constitution primarily because they were opposed to a strong central government. They believed a strong central government headed by a president could become a monarchy. Consequently, they favored a small central government that respected and defended the rights of individual states.

4. Roy P. Basler, ed., with Critical and Analytical Notes, Preface by Carl Sandburg, *Abraham Lincoln: His Speeches and Writings* (Cleveland: The World Publishing Company, 1946), 372-3.
5. Basler, ed., *Abraham Lincoln: His Speeches and Writings*, 1946, 734.
6. George Rogers Taylor, *The Transportation Revolution, 1815-1860* (New York: Holt, Rinehart and Winston, 1951), 174-75.

References:

Alden, John R. *George Washington: A Biography*. Baton Rouge: Louisiana State University Press, 1970.

Ammon, Harry. *James Monroe: The Quest for National Identity*. Hartford, Conn.: American Political Biography Press, 1998.

Bailyn, Bernard. *The Origins of American Politics*. New York: Vintage Books, 1970.

Baldwin, Leland D. *Whiskey Rebels: The Story of a Frontier Uprising*. Pittsburgh: University of Pittsburgh Press, 1939.

Barnard, Harry. *Rutherford B. Hayes and His America*. Indianapolis: Bobbs-Merrill, 1954.

Bauer, K. Jack. *Zachary Taylor: Soldier, Planter, Statesman of the Old Southwest*. Baton Rouge: Louisiana State University Press, 1993.

Billington, Ray A. *Westward Expansion: A History of the American Frontier* (2nd ed.). New York: Macmillan, 1960.

Boorstin, Daniel J. *The Americans: The National Experience*. New York: Random House, 1965.

Borneman, Walter R. *Polk: The Man Who Transformed the Presidency and America*. New York: Random House Trade Paperbacks, 2009.

Brands, H. W. *Andrew Jackson: His Life and Times*. New York: Anchor, 2006.

Brodsky, Alyn. *Grover Cleveland: A Study in Character*. New York: Truman Talley Books, 2000.

Burlingame, Michael. *Abraham Lincoln: A Life*. Baltimore: The Johns Hopkins University Press, 2009.

Burns, James McGregor. *The American Experiment: The Workshop of Democracy*. New York: Knopf, 1985.

Calloway, Colin G. *Crown and Calumet: British-Indian Relations, 1783-1815*. Norman, OK: Oklahoma Press, 1987.

Chernow, Ron. *Grant*. New York: Penguin Press, 2017.

Chernow, Ron. *The House of Morgan: An American Banking Dynasty and the Rise of Modern American Finance*. New York: Grove Press, 1990.

Chernow, Ron. *Washington: A Life*. New York: Penguin Press, 2010.

Chitwood, Oliver P. *John Tyler: Champion of the Old South*. Hartford, CT: American Political Biography Press, 1990.

Cleaves, Freeman. *Old Tippecanoe: William Henry Harrison and His Time*. New York: Charles Scribner's Sons, 1939.

Cochran, Thomas C. *Frontiers of Change: Early Industrialism in America*. New York: Oxford University Press, 1981.

Cole, Donald B. *Martin Van Buren and the American Political System*. Princeton, N.J.: Princeton University Press, 2016.

Cresson, W. P. *James Monroe*. Chapel Hill: The University of North Carolina Press, 1946.

Cunningham, Noble E. *In Pursuit of Reason: The Life of Thomas Jefferson*. Baton Rouge: Louisiana State University Press, 1987.

Davis, Burke. *Sherman's March*. New York: Random House, 1985.

Davis, William C. *Jefferson Davis: the Man and His Hour*. Baton Rouge: Louisiana State University Press, 1991.

Donald, David Herbert. *Lincoln*. New York: Simon & Schuster, 1995.

Doenecke, Justus D. *The Presidencies of James A. Garfield & Chester A. Arthur*. Lawrence: Regents Press of Kansas, 1981.

Douglass, Frederick. *Narrative of the Life of Frederick Douglass*. New York: Signet, 1968.

Ellis, Joseph J. *His Excellency: George Washington*. New York: Knopf, 2004.

Ellis, Joseph J. *Passionate Sage: The Character and Legacy of John Adams*. New York: W. W. Norton, 1994.

Ferling, John E. *John Adams: A Life*. Hartford, Conn.: American Political Biography Press, 1997.

Flexner, James Thomas. *George Washington: Anguish and Farewell, 1793-1799*. Boston: Little, Brown and Co., 1972.

Flexner, James Thomas. *George Washington and the New Nation: 1783-1793*. Boston: Little, Brown and Co., 1970.

Flexner, James Thomas. *Washington: The Indispensable Man*. Boston: Little, Brown, 1969.

Foner, Eric. *Reconstruction: America's Unfinished Revolution*. New York: Harper & Row, 1988.

Foner, Eric. *A Short History of Reconstruction, 1863-1877*. New York: Harper Collins, 1990.

Foote, Shelby. *The Civil War: A Narrative* (3 vols.). New York: Random House, 1958-74.

Franklin, John Hope. *From Slavery to Freedom*. New York: Knopf, 1974.

Freeman, Douglas S. *George Washington: A Biography*. New York: Charles Scribner's Sons, 1985.

Greenberger, Scott S. *The Unexpected President: The Life and Times of Chester A. Arthur*. New York: Da Capo Press, 2019.

Hecht, Marie B. *John Quincy Adams: A Personal History of an Independent Man*. Hartford, Conn.: American Political Biography Press, 1995.

Heckman, R. A. *Lincoln v. Douglas: the Great Debates Campaign.* Washington, D.C.: Public Affairs Press, 1967.

Hofstadter, Richard. *The American Political Tradition: And the Men Who Made It*, New York: Knopf, 1973.

Hofstadter, Richard. *The Idea of a Party System, 1780-1840.* Berkeley: University of California Press, 1970.

Hoogenboom, Ari. *Rutherford B. Hayes: Warrior and President.* Lawrence: University Press of Kansas, 1995.

Howe, G. F. *Chester A. Arthur: A Quarter-Century of Machine Politics.* New York: Dodd, Mead & Co., 1934.

Jahoda, Gloria. *The Trail of Tears: The Story of the American Indian Removal, 1813-1855.* New York: Holt, Rinehart and Winston, 1975.

Jeffers, H. P. *An Honest President: The Life and Presidencies of Grover Cleveland.* New York: William Morrow, 2000.

Johannsen, Robert. W. *Stephen A. Douglas.* New York: Oxford University Press, 1973.

Keller, Morton. *Affairs of State: Public Life in Late Nineteenth Century America.* Cambridge, Mass.: Belknap Press of Harvard University Press, 1977.

Ketcham, Ralph. *James Madison: A Biography.* Charlottesville: University of Virginia Press, 1990.

Kirkland, Edward Chase. *Dream and Thought in the Business Community, 1860-1900.* Ithaca, N.Y.: Cornell University Press, 1956.

Klein, Philip S. *President James Buchanan: A Biography.* Hartford, CT: American Political Biography Press, 1995.

Leahy, Christopher J. *President Without a Party: The Life of John Tyler.* Baton Rouge: Louisiana State University Press, 2020.

Leech, Margaret. *The Garfield Orbit.* New York: Harper & Row, 1978.

Leech, Margaret. *In the Days of McKinley.* Hartford, CT: American Political Biography Press, 1999.

Lewis, David Levering. *W. E. B. Du Bois: A Biography of a Race, 1868-1919.* New York: Henry Holt, 1993.

Long, Clarence D. *Wages and Earnings in the United States: 1860-1890.* Princeton, N. J.: Princeton University Press, 1960.

Malone, Dumas. *Jefferson and His Times* (6 vols.). Boston: Little, Brown, 1948-81.

May, Ernest R. *The Making of the Monroe Doctrine.* Cambridge, Mass.: Harvard University Press, 1975.

May, Gary. *John Tyler.* New York: Times Books, 2006.

McCullough, David. *John Adams.* New York: Simon & Schuster, 2001.

McCullough, David. *The Path Between the Seas: The Creation of the Panama Canal, 1870-1914.* New York: Simon & Schuster, 1977.

McFeely, William E. *Grant: A Biography.* New York: W. W. Norton, 1981.

McPherson, James M. *Battle Cry of Freedom: The Civil War Era*. London: Oxford University Press, 1988.

Merry, Robert W. *A Country of Vast Designs: James K. Polk, the Mexican War and the Conquest of the American Continent*. New York: Simon & Schuster, 2010.

Milton, George F. *The Age of Hate: Andrew Johnson and the Radicals*. New York: Coward McCann, 1930.

Mitchell, B. *Alexander Hamilton* (2 vols.). New York: Macmillan, 1957-62.

Morgan, Edmund S. *The Genius of George Washington*. New York: W. W. Norton, 1980.

Morgan, H. Wayne. *William McKinley and His America*. Syracuse, N.Y.: Syracuse University Press, 1963.

Morison, Samuel Eliot. *The Oxford History of the United States, 1783-1917*. London: Oxford University Press, 1982.

Nagel, Paul C. *John Quincy Adams: A Public Life, a Private Life*. Boston: Harvard University Press, 1999.

Nevins, Allan. *Grover Cleveland: A Study in Courage: to the Loss of the Presidency, 1837-1888*. Hartford, CT: American Political Biography Press, 2001.

Nichols, Roy F. *Franklin Pierce* (2nd ed.). Philadelphia: University of Pennsylvania Press, 1958.

Oates, Stephen B. *With Malice Toward None: The Life of Abraham Lincoln*. New York: Harper & Row, 1977.

Painter, Nell Irvin. *Standing at Armageddon: The United States, 1877-1919*. New York: W. W. Norton, 1987.

Paludan, Phillip S. *The Presidency of Abraham Lincoln*. Lawrence: University Press of Kansas, 1994.

Peskin, Allan. *Garfield*. Kent, Ohio: The Kent State University Press, 1978.

Peterson, Merrill D. *Thomas Jefferson and the New Nation: A Biography*. New York: Oxford University Press, 1975.

Pletcher, David M. *The Diplomacy of Annexation: Texas, Oregon and the Mexican War*. Columbia: University of Missouri Press, 1973.

Porter, Glenn. *The Rise of Big Business, 1860-1910*. New York: Thomas Y. Crowell, 1973.

Rakove, Jack N. *James Madison and the Creation of the American Republic*. New York: Longman, 2002.

Rayback, Robert J. *Millard Fillmore: Biography of a President*. Hartford, CT: American Political Biography Press, 1992.

Reeves, Thomas C. *Gentleman Boss: The Life of Chester Alan Arthur*. Hartford, CT: American Political Biography Press, 1991.

Remini, Robert V. *Andrew Jackson: The Course of American Democracy, 1833-1845*. Baltimore: The Johns Hopkins University Press, 1998.

Remini, Robert V. *Andrew Jackson: The Course of American Empire, 1767-1821*. Baltimore: The Johns Hopkins University Press, 1998.

Remini, Robert V. *Andrew Jackson: The Course of American Freedom, 1822-1832*. Baltimore: The Johns Hopkins University Press, 1998.

Remini, Robert V. *Henry Clay: Statesman for the Union*. New York: W. W. Norton, 1991.

Remini, Robert V. *The Life of Andrew Jackson*. New York: Harper Perennial Modern Classics, 2010.

Remini, Robert V. *Martin Van Buren and the Making of the Democratic Party*. New York: W. W. Norton, 1959.

Rogin, Michael P. *Fathers and Children: Andrew Jackson and the Destruction of the American Indians*. New York: Knopf, 1975.

Rutland, Robert A. *James Madison: The Founding Father*. New York: Macmillan, 1987.

Schlesinger, Arthur M. *The Age of Jackson*. New York: Back Bay Books, 1988.

Sellers, Charles G. *James K. Polk* (2 vols.). Princeton, N.J.: Princeton University Press, 1957-66.

Sievers, Harry J. *Benjamin Harrison: Hoosier President*. Hartford, CT: American Political Biography Press, 1996.

Sievers, Harry J. *Benjamin Harrison: Hoosier Statesman*. Hartford, CT: American Political Biography Press, 1997.

Sievers, Harry J. *Benjamin Harrison: Hoosier Warrior*. Hartford, CT: American Political Biography Press, 1997.

Smith, Elbert B. *The Presidencies of Zachary Taylor and Millard Fillmore*. Lawrence: University Press of Kansas, 1988.

Smith, Jean Edward. *Grant*. New York: Simon & Schuster, 2002.

Smith, Page. *John Adams* (2 vols.). New York: Doubleday, 1962.

Socolofsky, Homer E. and Allan Spetter. *The Presidency of Benjamin Harrison*. Lawrence: University Press of Kansas, 1987.

Stampp, Kenneth M. *The Peculiar Institution: Slavery in the Anti-Bellum South*. New York: Knopf, 1956.

Stewart, David O. *Impeached: The Trial of President Andrew Johnson and the Fight for Lincoln's Legacy*. New York: Simon & Schuster, 2010.

Taylor, George Rogers and Irene D. Neu. *The American Railroad Network, 1861-90*. Cambridge, Mass.: Harvard University Press, 1956.

Taylor, George Rogers. *Transportation Revolution, 1815-1860*. New York: Rinehart & Co., 1951.

Thomas, Emory M. *Robert E. Lee: A Biography*. New York: W. W. Norton, 1995.

Trefousse, Hans L. *Andrew Johnson: A Biography*. New York: W. W. Norton, 1989.

Unger, Harlow Giles. *John Quincy Adams*. New York: Da Capo Press, 2013.

Unger, Harlow Giles. *The Last Founding Father: James Monroe and a Nation's Call to Greatness*. New York: Da Capo Press, 2009.

Wade, Wyn Craig. *The Fiery Cross: The Ku Klux Klan in America*. New York: Simon & Schuster, 1987.

Wallner, Peter A. *Franklin Pierce: Martyr for the Union*. Concord, N.H.:Plaidswede Pub. Co., 2007.

Wallner, Peter A. *Franklin Pierce: New Hampshire's Favorite Son*. Concord, N.H.: Plaidswede Pub. Co., 2004.

Welch, Richard E., Jr. *The Presidencies of Grover Cleveland*. Lawrence: University Press of Kansas, 1988.

White, Ronald C. *A. Lincoln: A Biography*. New York: Random House, 2009.

Williams, John Hoyt. *A Great and Shining Road: The Epic Story of the Transcontinental Railroad*. New York: Times Books, 1988.

Wilson, Edmund. *Patriotic Gore: Studies in the Literature of the American Civil War*. New York: Oxford University Press, 1962.

Woodward, C. Vann. *Reunion and Reaction: The Compromise of 1877 and the End of Reconstruction*. Boston: Little, Brown, 1966.

Wright, Edmund. *Franklin of Philadelphia*. Cambridge, Mass.: Harvard University Press, 1986.

Chapter 4

Political and Social Change in the United States from 1901 to 1960

McKinley, who had been elected in 1896, easily defeated his Democratic opponent, William Jennings Bryan, in 1900, and American imperialism, although bleak, emerged. The nation prospered. Unfortunately, many in government believed big business controlled the country.

Because McKinley's vice-president, Garret A. Hobart, had died, Theodore Roosevelt was now vice-president. In 1901 McKinley was shot by Leon Czolgosz, an anarchist, and died several days later.

Theodore Roosevelt became president.

Roosevelt had been born in New York City and had graduated from Harvard University. He had served as police commissioner of New York City. In 1889 he had become a member of the United States Civil Service Commission. By this time he had written several books about American history and other subjects. He had served as the assistant secretary of the United States Navy. He and the Rough Riders had served during the Spanish-American War. He had been elected governor of New York and in 1900 had become vice-president.

Progressivism was a result of various groups actively responding to problems caused by the Industrial Revolution. These problems included poverty caused primarily by low wages and too many members in a family as well as slums caused by too many immigrants and/or low-income families living together. Slums were also caused by slum-lords who refused to prepare or improve their property.

Collusion between businessmen and politicians had a negative effect on the American political process. The growth of monopolized industries not only defied the Sherman Anti-Trust Act, but angered the citizenry. Consequently, various movements appeared and each was for reform or reconstruction. Usually, the goals for each movement were the same: enact legislation that would help the poor, eliminate collusion between politicians and business leaders, control monopolization, and enable the citizenry—every citizen of the United States—to participate in the welfare of the nation.

Different groups—political, professional, and religious—were making demands, and in city after city some of their demands were met. For instance, corrupt politicians were voted out of office; slum districts were improved; the poor were helped; taxation of industries was increased; legislation to help labor was enacted; legislation to improve education was passed; and legislation which affected every voting registrant was enacted. The Progressive Movement was prevalent in the United States.

Needless to say, Roosevelt, even though he was a Republican, was a progressive president. He sympathized with the various movements and immediately acted on their behalf. A strong advocate for reform, he reactivated the Sherman Anti-Trust Act and attempted to regulate what had become known as trusts, which had been created by businesses and industries for the purpose of manipulating prices in more than one product category, among other questionable practices. He denounced J. P. Morgan, U. S. Steel, John D. Rockefeller, and Standard Oil, among other individuals and companies. He was responsible for the dissolution of the Northern Securities Company, which included railroads and other companies overseen by wealthy businessmen and financiers who had escaped being regulated by the federal government primarily because few, if any, laws existed that controlled trusts. Roosevelt gained the public's support by reacting to public outcry. Instead of trying to appease the public through speeches like many politicians, including presidents, he acted.

Roosevelt's administration represented the population of the nation. For instance, he had individuals from different minorities serving in positions.

Roosevelt had been a sickly child and had enjoyed the outdoors. Later, after his first wife died, he had journeyed to the Badlands and had purchased a ranch, where he had lived and worked. In his spare time he had hunted wild game. Roosevelt had grown to love the land. After a few years, he had returned home and had married his second wife. Still, thoughts about the West entered his mind. Conserving it for later generations became important to him. Consequently, as president, he eagerly supported legislation that protected vast areas of land.

In 1902, when the United Mine Workers went on strike, Roosevelt intervened on their behalf. In fact, he threatened to have the United States Army take over the mines, which caused the mine owners to compromise and the miners to return to work.

A year later he encouraged Congress to pass the Elkins Act, which regulated railroads.

In 1904 he defeated Judge Alton Parker, a Democrat, and was elected president. Because most members of Congress were Republicans as well, he was able to sign additional reform legislation. However, when he supported bills that would regulate rates charged by railroads, he was opposed by members of his own party. They also did not like his support of the Pure Food and Drug Act and the Meat Inspection Act. These two acts passed after several articles by muckraking journalists like Samuel Hopkins Adams and Upton Sinclair exposed the dangers of patent medicine and the unsanitary conditions in meat-packing plants.

In 1906 he persuaded Congress to pass the Hepburn Act, which provided power to the Interstate Commerce Commission. As a result, the commission set maximum rates for railroads.

Roosevelt helped establish the Department of Commerce and Labor with a Bureau of Corporations. He was instrumental in the establishment of a Public Lands Commission and a National Conservation Commission, among others. Roosevelt favored workmen's compensation, income taxes, and the regulation of the stock market. He opposed child labor.

More than any other president, he was responsible for the Panama Canal becoming a reality.

Roosevelt received the Nobel Peace Prize for his tireless efforts in the settlement of the Russo-Japanese War. However, he was criticized for his expansionist policies.

After two terms Roosevelt selected his successor, William Howard Taft, as the Republican candidate for president.

Taft defeated William Jennings Bryan, a Democrat, in 1908.

Taft had been born in Ohio and had been educated at Yale University. He had served in various political positions, including secretary of war under President Roosevelt.

As president, Taft thought he could follow in his predecessor's footsteps, but he was too conservative to be a progressive. Republicans who were progressives asked for additional measures to regulate railroads and corporations, a lower tariff, and an income tax, among other legislation. Unfortunately, Taft's legislation, specifically, the Payne-Aldrich Act, affected the tariff very little. In fact, the bill helped industries and hurt consumers. Such legislation only angered the progressives, and consequently the party split. Without question, Taft disappointed Roosevelt. Instead of introducing regulations against monopolies like Standard Oil, Taft used anti-trust suits. He also dismissed Gifford Pinchot, head of the Division of Forestry (now the Forest Service), because he disagreed with Pinchot about how the division should be managed. Pinchot had been chosen by Roosevelt.

In 1910 the Democrats passed several progressive bills that caused voters to elect more Democrats to the House of Representatives and the Senate of the United States. Taft's conservative position, not to mention his authorization to sell public land to wealthy syndicates, deepened his party's separation.

In 1912 Roosevelt attempted to defeat Taft at the Republican National Convention, but he was not successful. Disappointed, he helped form the Progressive Party, which became known as the Bull Moose Party, and campaigned on a platform called the New Nationalism. Although he opposed Taft and Woodrow Wilson, a Democrat, he failed to win the presidency primarily because he and Taft split the Republican Party and voters.

Woodrow Wilson, a Democrat who had campaigned on a platform called the New Freedom, became president.

Later, Taft taught law at the Yale Law School and in 1921 was appointed Chief Justice of the Supreme Court of the United States.

Woodrow Wilson was perhaps the most formally educated president in the nation's history. (Of course, the reader must remember that the founders of the nation lived during the Age of Enlightenment and consequently had read works by the greatest minds of the period.) A Calvinist, Wilson was guided by his religious beliefs and his formal education. However, he was not stuffy. Like Lincoln, he enjoyed telling humorous stories.

Wilson had taught in more than one university and had written about history and government before he had served as the president of Princeton University. As a Democrat, he had been elected governor of New Jersey in 1910. Two years later the Democrats had nominated him for president. He had heard about so-called bosses—individuals who had controlled cities—but he had never been intimidated by any. Even those who ran the Democratic Party could not manipulate him.

As president, Wilson had the support of the House of Representatives and the Senate of the United States primarily because most of the members of both chambers were Democrats. Consequently, his New Freedom policies were not only entertained by Congress, but passed.

The Sixteenth and Seventeenth Amendments, which had been supported by former President Taft, were ratified and became law when Wilson occupied the White House. The Sixteenth Amendment allowed the federal government to enact an income tax. (The reader must remember that the federal government could enact an income tax, which it did.)[1] The Seventeenth Amendment stipulated that senators had to be elected by the people, not appointed by state legislatures.

Wilson, unlike previous presidents, held regular press conferences, but he was not very candid with the reporters who attended. Still, he was able to persuade Congress that the federal government needed to become larger in order to become more benevolent.

The Underwood Tariff Act, which removed the protection industries had enjoyed, was signed in 1913. As a result, businesses at home had to compete with businesses abroad. Prices on numerous products were lowered. The same year the Federal Reserve Act, which was a result of banks closing during the panic of 1907, was passed. This act created a federal reserve system overseen by a federal reserve board. The new monetary system, which included Reserve Banks, issued federal reserve notes based on gold and commercial paper. The banking structure of the United States subsequently changed and dramatically improved. However, this act caused Jacksonian Democrats to question Wilson's political party affiliation. After all, former President Jackson had opposed the Bank of the United States. Some Democrats realized that Wilson was not only liberal, but too progressive for the country's welfare.

In 1914 the Federal Trade Commission, which was empowered to investigate questionable business practices, including monopolistic practices, was established. The same year the Clayton Anti-Trust Act was passed. This act, which supported the Sherman Anti-Trust Act of 1890, encouraged competition and protected labor unions from anti-trust litigation.

In 1916 the Federal Farm Loan Act and the Adamson Act were passed. The former provided inexpensive loans to farmers. The latter introduced the eight-hour work day primarily to railroad employees.

Wilson tried to exhibit his abilities in foreign policy, too. His secretary of state, William Jennings Bryan, negotiated treaties with other countries in Europe, including Great Britain, to forestall war until investigations were made to determine whether war was necessary to alleviate differences. Unfortunately, the countries went to war after the treaties' obligations were met.

Although World War I had started in Europe in 1914, Wilson had been opposed to the United States becoming involved. In fact, he had issued a proclamation of neutrality. When American businesses, farmers, and financiers began to support the Allied Nations, it was evident that the United States was not necessarily neutral. When Germany sank the *Lusitania*, a passenger ship, in 1915, German officials assured Wilson that such incidents would not happen in the future.

In 1916 Wilson ran for reelection, promising Americans that the nation would stay out of the war. Charles Evans Hughes, a former governor of New York and an associate justice of the Supreme Court of the United States, was a formidable Republican candidate, but Wilson defeated him.

In 1917 Germany increased its war at sea, sinking more ships, including several cargo ships from the United States bound for Great Britain. Germany had broken its word. Several months later, Wilson asked Congress for a declaration of war.

Nationalization of railroads, and controls over industry, laborers, food, and petroleum products immediately passed through Congress. Wilson saw the Espionage Act and the Selective Service Act pass through Congress in 1917. Before the war officially ended in 1919, Wilson presented his Fourteen Points. Then he presented his Four Principles and finally his Five Particulars. All spelled out his plan for peace. For instance, he desired for the United States to have treaties with other nations. In addition, he desired for the United States to join what the British called the League of Nations. Congress worked on several of the points he had presented, but it did not approve joining the so-called League of Nations.

Wilson was awarded the Nobel Peace Prize in 1919.

Although Wilson had personal advisors, he enjoyed being around certain women, especially his first wife, Ellen, and his second wife, Edith. In fact, after Wilson suffered several strokes in 1919, which left him paralyzed on the left side, Edith not only protected him, but more than likely made presidential decisions based on what he had told her.

Before the next presidential election, the Eighteenth Amendment, which prohibited alcohol from being made and sold, was ratified. However, alcohol was made and sold illegally. Gangsters bootlegged it to so-called speakeasies and individuals made it in bathtubs or makeshift stills.

In 1920 the Nineteenth Amendment, which gave women the right to vote, was added to the constitution.

The Democrats nominated James M. Cox for president. The Republicans nominated Warren G. Harding. Primarily because Harding was a conservative who believed the United States was the greatest country in the world, he called for normality, which would dramatically curtail progressivism. Without question, Americans liked Harding. Indeed, they voted for him almost two to one. His Electoral College votes were at an even greater percentage.

Harding had been born in Ohio. He had published a newspaper in Marion, Ohio, and had been involved in other businesses as well. He had been elected to the United States Senate in 1914 and had favored protective tariffs for businesses and had supported the United States in World War I. However, he had been opposed to the League of Nations.

As president, Harding appointed respected statesmen and successful businessmen to his cabinet. In 1921 he supported the Budget and Accounting Act that established the Bureau of the Budget and the General Accounting Office, which improved the budgeting practices of the federal government. In short, it controlled government expenditures that soon ended an economic recession. However, it enabled the first director, Charles G. Dawes, to economize even at the expense of the public's welfare. In 1922 the Fordney-McCumber Act was passed by Congress. This act helped manufacturers, but did little for farmers. Harding's administration apparently was against labor because it allowed lower wages. It also interfered in strikes.

In 1923 Harding learned that the director of the Veterans Bureau had been selling government supplies at low prices and that the secretary of the interior had earned several hundred thousand dollars from selling leases of government land to oil companies. The latter scandal became known as Teapot Dome, which was the name that had been given to the oil reserve in Wyoming. Eventually, Albert D. Fall, the secretary of the interior, was charged for accepting bribes and sentenced to prison. Although Harding, himself, had brought a sense of normality to the country, Fall and several other individuals who had made up Harding's cabinet tarnished him and his administration.

Later the same year, while touring the nation, Harding suffered a heart attack and died. Calvin Coolidge, his vice-president, was at his father's farm when he heard the news and was sworn in as president.

As mentioned, a few members of Harding's cabinet were involved in money-making schemes that tarnished his presidency. After his death, several so-called journalists wrote articles and books about

Harding and his involvement in the scandals that became public. However, the allegations made in these articles and books were based on lies and the writers' imaginations, not necessarily facts. Indeed, Harding was never charged for any wrong-doing.

Calvin Coolidge had been born in Vermont and had graduated from Amherst College. He had practiced law in Massachusetts and had served as governor of the state. He had successfully handled the Boston Police Strike of 1919 by relying on the rule of law. He had been elected vice-president under Harding in 1920.

As president, Coolidge brought integrity to the White House. Overall, he approved of cutting regulations for businesses and industries and opposed federal aid to farmers. For instance, he vetoed the McNary-Haugen Farm Relief Act that would have helped the farmer as much as the nation.

He strongly believed in businesses regulating themselves, so the federal government would not have to get involved. He favored lower taxes, too, which helped every working American. Although he would not speak for what seemed like hours, he was a very good listener.

In 1924 he defeated John W. Davis, a Democrat, and Robert La Follette, a Progressive. To say the least, the country enjoyed stability and prosperity while Coolidge was president. Indeed, millions of couples purchased houses, not to mention products like radios and automobiles. However, as mentioned, Coolidge was interested in helping businesses, not necessarily farmers. He was not interested in governmental or social reform, either. Of course, not all of his policies were acceptable to Congress. The policies that became legislation may or may not have affected the growth and prosperity of the country. After all, production of various products had improved. Indeed, the cost to produce a product had lowered as a result of fewer parts or fewer steps or processes being involved. In short, manufacturers were developing newer methods all the time. When profits increased, new plants were constructed. Coincidentally, wages increased, but so did profits. Whether labor was harmed by Coolidge's policies depends on one's perspective.

During Coolidge's presidency, primarily because his administration's policies toward the stock market were weak, several unscrupulous so-called businessmen created companies for the purpose of selling stocks to people who did not know anything about the companies or the stocks. Other corporations' stocks increased in value at astronomical rates. Investors borrowed money to buy stock—stock which they believed would not only enable them to pay their loans but earn a profit. Unfortunately, his administration reveled in the country's growth instead of limiting credit.

Coolidge allowed privately owned utility companies to merge by failing to pass responsible legislation. Thus the cost of electricity increased in parts of the country. As a result, some thought he was irresponsible.

If people put their money in banks and the banks failed, peoples' savings were not necessarily insured. In addition, most people who worked had no financial security if they were laid off, or, worse, lost their jobs altogether. These problems were discussed as well.

In 1928 Coolidge did not seek reelection. Instead, he wrote his autobiography, which was published a year later.

Herbert C. Hoover had been born in Iowa and had graduated from Stanford University. A mining engineer who had traveled extensively throughout the world, he had served as the head of the United States Food Administration, which had been established primarily to stabilize the price of wheat, during World War I. This became the American Relief Administration in 1919. Hoover's humanitarian efforts had been credited for saving millions of lives throughout Europe. President Warren Harding had appointed him secretary of commerce. Hoover's conservatism had been appreciated by leaders of the Republican Party. In 1928 they had nominated him for president. The Democrats had nominated Alfred E. Smith, governor of New York and an opponent of prohibition. Hoover defeated Smith, the first Catholic to run for president.

President Hoover was informed that excessive speculation in the stock market had caused stock prices to become inflated. Although he warned leaders in New York, he did not take any action. The stock market crashed in 1929 and caused the Great Depression. Almost immediately, various members of Congress encouraged Hoover to act.

The leading economists at the time suggested that nothing be done, that the Great Depression should be allowed to run its course.[2] More than likely this is the reason President Hoover was reluctant to sign more bills than what he signed while serving as president. Of course, President Hoover was criticized for doing little, when, in reality, he did more than most people realized at the time. Those who knew he had taken action believed his action was too subtle for the crisis at hand, however.

President Hoover attempted to persuade business leaders to keep their respective businesses and industries operating and maintain wages. He encouraged business leaders to keep employees working.

At Hoover's urging, Congress passed the Agriculture Marketing Act that established the Federal Farm Board, which stabilized farm prices.

Unfortunately, he signed the Smoot-Hawley Tariff Act of 1930, which was similar to the Fordney-McCumber Tariff Act of 1922. Sadly, this act did not help matters. Indeed, both protected manufacturers in the United States by basically prohibiting companies in Europe from competing, which caused prices to remain high. In short, had companies in Europe been allowed to compete with companies in the United States, prices of many products would have decreased and as a result more people would have been able to purchase more goods. Instead, the Smoot-Hawley Tariff Act caused nations in Europe to put tariffs on goods manufactured in the United States, which contributed to the depression in the United States.

Small banks and businesses started failing before 1931. Although several programs were mentioned to him as possible remedies, he rejected them. Hoover tried to restore Americans' faith in the capitalistic system, but Americans were discouraged. Hoover believed that most of the problems had started in Europe, not in the United States.

Indeed, Germany's economy was faltering just like other European countries at the time. If Germany's economy failed, other European nations would be effected. In order to save Germany, Hoover agreed to a one-year moratorium on war-dept payments. The nations in Europe had borrowed from the United States during World War I, but none were in a position to make payments. Unfortunately, depositors in

England and other European nations started removing their money from banks. As if this was not grave enough, these countries went off of the gold standard. The United States did not.

Hoover signed the Emergency Relief and Construction Act in 1932, which established the Reconstruction Finance Corporation that provided funding for public works projects. The same year the Federal Home Loan Bank Act was passed to establish the Federal Home Loan Bank Board and the Federal Home Loan Banks, which provided loans to banks, building and loan associations, insurance companies, and other financial institutions that financed mortgages for houses.

Congress passed the Glass-Steagall Act of 1932, which allowed the Federal Reserve Bank to provide loans to other banks in the system and to issue Federal Reserve Bank Notes. However, this act was for emergency situations.

As Hoover increased government spending, several members of Congress believed too much federal money was going out. In 1932 Congress passed the Revenue Act. Hoover signed the bill and watched as taxes on businesses and individuals increase.

As more money flowed into the system, it decreased in value. In short, the inflation rate grew higher faster. Of course, the administration was trying to stimulate the market, but such measures did not necessarily work.

If the federal government had removed the protective tariffs several years before 1929, perhaps the depression would not have been as grave.

As if these measures were not bad enough, Hoover had to order General Douglas MacArthur to evict an army of veterans who had come to Washington, D. C., to encourage Congress to pay the bonus that had been promised to them earlier than the assigned date. As a result of General MacArthur's military action against the veterans, Hoover and his administration received negative coverage by the press.

Before he left office, Hoover saw the nation's banking system almost collapse. Across the country thousands of banks closed their doors for good. Businesses and industries that had been financially sound a few years before had become bankrupt. Stocks—those that had any value—were worth considerably less than what they originally cost.

Cities and states needed revenue to pay their various employees, but revenue was difficult to obtain. Many Americans were unemployed and many were destitute.

In 1932 the Republicans re-nominated Hoover, but he was defeated by Franklin Delano Roosevelt, a Democrat, who had promised a New Deal. The Democrats also won the House of Representatives and the Senate of the United States.

Hoover returned to government service in the 1940s and again in the 1950s. He chaired two commissions that studied governmental organization.

Franklin Delano Roosevelt had been born in New York and had attended the Groton School, Harvard University, and the Columbia University Law School. Although a distant relative of Theodore Roosevelt, he disagreed with Theodore when it came to governmental policy. For instance, Franklin had supported President Wilson's policies and had served in his administration as the assistant secretary of the United States Navy.

In 1920 James M. Cox, a Democrat, had been nominated for president. Franklin had been nominated for vice-president. However, Cox lost the presidency. A year later Franklin had contracted poliomyelitis while on vacation in Canada and subsequently could not walk without support. However, this disease had not ended his political aspirations. In 1928 he had been elected governor of New York.

In 1932 the Democrats had nominated Franklin for president. Primarily because the United States, like other countries around the world, had faced an economic depression, Franklin had easily defeated President Hoover.

As president, Roosevelt used radio to reach the American people. He used these so-called "fireside chats" to inform listeners about different aspects of the economy and about his so-called New Deal programs, which, hopefully, would get the nation out of the Great Depression. The New Deal programs addressed different aspects of the economy, including banking, the stock market, farming, and the unemployed. At the time Roosevelt entered the White House, almost 25 percent of the country's workforce was unemployed.

In 1933 Roosevelt encouraged Congress to pass several bills. For instance, Congress hastily passed the Emergency Banking Relief Act, which provided a brief holiday for the banks in an effort to prevent more people from withdrawing their money. This act also called for examiners to inspect banks to make certain they were financially sound before they reopened. The Government Economy Act cut salaries of federal employees, including those in the military, and decreased federal government spending. Roosevelt persuaded Congress to pass the Beer-Wine Revenue Act, which allowed wine and beer to be sold and, more important, to be taxed. Of course, this act was soon followed by the passage of the Twenty-First Amendment, which ended Prohibition. Apparently, President Roosevelt and members of Congress realized that Prohibition had caused the federal government to lose revenue. Besides, because many people desired some form of liquor, corrupt politicians along with organized crime figures had supplied it. Consequently, the federal government had to hire agents to investigate possible corruption between politicians and organized crime figures or syndicates as well as those who actually produced beer and liquor. This is not including the amount the federal government had lost from taxes on alcoholic beverages.

The Civilian Conservation Corporation was created in 1933 primarily to hire young workers, including veterans, to plant forests and maintain roads and trails in wooded areas.

In 1933 the Federal Emergency Relief Act, which created the Federal Emergency Relief Administration (FERA), was passed. This act provided grants rather than loans to states primarily to fund jobs in agriculture, construction, and other areas. The same year the Agricultural Adjustment Act established the Agricultural Adjustment Administration, which set minimum prices for the major agricultural products, including crops, beef, and pork. If necessary, it limited or curtailed the major agricultural products, too, in order to achieve the prices. In short, this caused prices for crops, beef, and pork to actually increase. When many

Americans learned about this, they were outraged. After all, many were out of work and consequently had very little or no income.[3]

The Emergency Farm Mortgage Act, which was passed in 1933, provided loans to farmers so they would not lose their farms. The Tennessee Valley Authority Act was passed the same year. This act established the Tennessee Valley Authority (TVA), which enabled the federal government to build hydroelectric power plants to produce electricity. In addition, the TVA built dams and developed recreational areas. Many leaders were opposed to the act because it allowed the federal government to build certain projects that normally would have been built by private enterprises. These leaders thought—and rightly so—that the federal government was interfering in American business. (Eventually, once the dams and the hydroelectric power plants were built, the federal government—through the TVA—actually competed against other businesses that produced electricity. Of course, the federal government had an advantage: it could keep its costs lower than the competition, which it did. In short, its customers were charged less.)

Still, President Roosevelt and Congress were not finished passing legislation in 1933. For instance, the Sale of Securities Act attempted to protect prospective investors by requiring corporations to provide information about their stocks. The Home Owners Refinancing Act established the Home Owners Loan Corporation, which refinanced mortgages to prevent foreclosures. The act also provided more funding to mortgage lenders. However, this corporation closed within a few years.

The Glass-Steagall Banking Act of 1933 established the Federal Deposit Insurance Corporation (FDIC), which banks joined and which protected depositors' savings accounts. In addition, investment banking was separated from retail banking. As a result, retail banks were regulated by the Federal Reserve. In addition, these banks could no longer use funds from depositors for investments that were considered risky.

The same year the National Industrial Recovery Act, which established the National Recovery Administration (NRA), was enacted primarily to raise prices on industrial goods. The overall aim of the act seemed sound. The federal government supported those businesses that guaranteed that production and prices would remain stable; the federal government supported those employees who worked for a minimum wage and a limited workday per week. Manufacturers increased production in anticipation of purchasing power, but the latter failed to materialize, and the program grew too complicated. Nonetheless, the act ended child labor, and overall working conditions improved greatly. The act also established the Public Works Administration, which hired independent contractors to build various projects such as bridges, dams, and tunnels, to mention a few. As a result, countless jobs were created for the unemployed. However, the program failed because too many codes had been implemented to regulate both industry and labor.

In 1934 Roosevelt and Congress initiated additional legislation, including the Loans to Industry Act, which extended the Reconstruction Finance Corporation that had been started by President Hoover.

The National Housing Act, which established the Federal Housing Administration, was passed the same year. The Federal Housing Administration provided federal insurance for mortgages, which protected lenders.

The Securities Exchange Act established the Securities and Exchange Commission. The act required Wall Street to disclose relevant information regarding new securities. In short, the Securities and Exchange Commission regulated stocks and the stock market. The Federal Communication Act was passed and provided the Federal Communications Commission with the charge of regulating the telephone, telegraph, and radio communications industries.

In 1935 the United States Supreme Court found a few of the acts, including the National Industrial Recovery Act and the Agricultural Adjustment Act, unconstitutional. As a result, whatever resulted from these acts were discontinued. Disgusted with the justices' decisions, President Roosevelt immediately submitted a bill to Congress that would increase the actual number of justices serving on the United States Supreme Court. (The possible reason for Roosevelt exhibiting such childish behavior is because he was spoiled as a child and as an adult. Indeed, he had been very close to his mother primarily because he had been her only child. Furthermore, as an adult, he was spoiled and protected by his wife and other women he had grown to love.) Fortunately, for the country, his supporters in Congress were forced to compromise, and the number of justices remained the same.

However, Roosevelt and his administration were not finished. In 1935 several acts were passed by Congress and signed into law. For instance, the Soil Conservation and Domestic Allotment Act, which basically subsidized farmers to plant soil-building crops such as beans, was passed. This act was in reaction to the so-called Dust Bowl that had been caused by drought and wind primarily in the central part of the country. Farmers and their tenants had lost crops. Consequently, many farmers had moved west.

The Emergency Relief Appropriation replaced the Federal Emergency Relief Act of 1933. The new bill funded the Works Progress Administration (WPA), which replaced the Public Works Administration. The Works Progress Administration was similar to its predecessor in that many unemployed people were hired to build airports, bridges, public buildings, public parks, roads, and schools. In addition, it funded artists who created works of art for public buildings and parks.

The Resettlement Act established the Resettlement Administration, which educated farmers about how to convert what was considered poor land for farming into land that would be suitable for farming.

The Social Security Act, which created the Social Security Trust Fund and Administration, was passed the same year. This act was attacked by members of Congress. For instance, Representative John Taber of New York said, "Never in the history of the world has any measure been brought in here so insidiously designed as to prevent business recovery, to enslave workers, and to prevent any possibility of the employers providing work for the people."[4] Prominent business leaders, including Alfred P. Sloan, Jr., who was the head of General Motors, and others, including many of the leading thinkers at the time, also criticized it. It should be mentioned that at the time the act provided income to the elderly, not necessarily the various groups it covers today.

President Roosevelt's popularity among the laboring class had increased as a result of his position toward the 1935 National Labor Relations Act or the Wagner Act, which was actually a broadening of the Norris-LaGuardia Act that President Hoover had signed. The act, which established the National Labor Relations Board, provided federal government protection to the rights of employees to organize and address working conditions, with or without union representation, and prohibited unfair practices by businesses. He was popular among others as well because of other legislation that had been enacted. Whether any of this legislation had an actual positive effect on the Great Depression is debatable. Of course, as a result of the federal government being responsible for creating new jobs, the unemployment figure had decreased to 16.9 percent before his first term ended. Consequently, President Roosevelt easily defeated Republican Governor Alfred M. Landon of Kansas in 1936.

Without question, President Roosevelt had initiated what became the foundation for a welfare state. Although the federal government had provided hope to many people by providing a temporary job and a temporary income, it now offered what would become a permanent welfare program. Initially, Social Security was supposed to provide a small pension to individuals based on what each had paid into it and it was not supposed to start until several years later, in 1942. However, Congress amended the date to 1940. Over the years Congress broadened the program. In addition to what has been mentioned, Social Security includes income to the elderly, the blind, the disabled or handicapped, and even the children in low-income households. It also provides health insurance for the elderly and the disabled or handicapped, housing for low-income families, job training, and other benefits. This act, more than any other, has led to the welfare state and has caused the problems the leading thinkers at the time warned about. When one examines the numerous progressive bills that have been passed by Congress and signed into law by presidents during the 1900s alone, there can be only one outcome: a welfare state that has caused the national debt to skyrocket. Of course, when bureaucratic entities are created by Congress, it is almost impossible for Congress to get rid of them. Yet, every bureaucratic entity created has to be funded.

In 1937, as the economy worsened, primarily because of President Roosevelt's decision to balance the budget, unemployment figures increased as production figures decreased. His commitment to the New Deal encouraged Congress to enact legislation for public works, the poor, the farmer, and the laborer. The United States Housing Act, which was the Wagner-Steagall Act, created the United States Housing Authority, which funded state-operated public housing projects. Of course, there were other pieces of legislation that passed, too, including the New Agricultural Adjustment Act, which replaced the Agricultural Adjustment Act of 1933 that had been ruled unconstitutional by the United States Supreme Court.

In 1938 the Fair Labor Standards Act, which established specific wages for certain kinds of work and actually encouraged the minimum wage and the maximum work week, was passed.

During the late 1930s, labor unions exercised their rights which ranged from enlisting thousands of members to organizing strikes. John L. Lewis, the president of the United Mine Workers of America, formed the Committee for Industrial Organization (CIO), which unionized the large mass-production industries. The American Federation of Labor (AFL) did the same. Of course, fights between unions and between unions and industries resulted. Workers were injured or killed in strikes. However, numerous companies eventually recognized the unions and their power for destroying lives and property. Of course, President Roosevelt and his administration reacted to such events by encouraging Congress to enact relevant legislation.

As a few intelligent journalists pointed out at the time, former President Hoover had started several programs that caused the federal government to become more involved in the nation's economy. However, President Roosevelt expanded the federal government's involvement by signing legislation for more expansive (and expensive) programs. Indeed, if one or more programs did not work, his administration came up with others. Unfortunately, many of his policies for businesses did not necessarily work. His policies for the federal government, especially those that provided jobs for building various projects such as airports, bridges, public buildings, and roads, among others, and the Tennessee Valley Authority, which brought electricity to areas of the country that had been overlooked, were successful but extremely expensive. For instance, when President Roosevelt entered the White House in 1933, the national debt was 22.5 billion dollars. By 1940, before the United States entered World War II, the national debt had increased to 42.9 billion dollars.

Although the press had reported about the economic problems in Europe, it now reported about Germany's military expansion into other countries. President Roosevelt discussed this problem as well with his advisors and cabinet members. Of course, the public's attitude in the United States was to stay out of any military conflict overseas. In fact, in 1935, the Neutrality Act was passed as Italy prepared to invade Ethiopia. The act restricted the sale of arms by American munitions manufacturers. The Neutrality Act was revised in 1939, when Germany invaded Poland, which actually sparked World War II.

President Roosevelt allowed Great Britain and France to purchase arms, but such aid did very little against Adolf Hitler's goal. When Hitler made a nonaggression pact with Joseph Stalin and Stalin attacked Finland, a country that paid off its debts from World War I, Roosevelt was appalled. Yet the two countries—Russia and Germany—did not halt their armies. Russia captured the Baltic republics and Germany invaded Denmark and Norway. Later, German forces captured the Netherlands, Belgium, and Luxembourg. Italy joined the German army when it invaded France, which eventually fell to Germany's prowess.

In 1940 President Roosevelt thought seriously about leaving the presidency. After all, he had served two terms. However, he was re-nominated by the Democrats. During the election, President Roosevelt promised that the United States would provide only aid to Great Britain, which faced fascism in Italy and National Socialism in Germany. More than likely he realized that the United States inevitably would be drawn into what would become World War II.

President Roosevelt defeated Wendell Willkie in 1940. Willkie actually held similar views on foreign policy as Roosevelt. In fact, like Roosevelt, he had been in favor of Congress passing the Selective Training and Service Act, which was the Burke-Wadsworth Act. Although leading members of Congress had argued about it, the act had passed in 1940 and had established the first peace-time selective service system in the United States.

Before 1941 President Roosevelt worked with Winston Churchill on what became the Atlantic Charter, which was the formal policy of the United States and Great Britain. In the early months of 1941, the Lend-Lease Act was passed. This act allowed England to wait until after the war before repaying what she borrowed from the United States. Munitions were sent immediately to Great Britain. As cargo ships crossed the Atlantic Ocean, a German U-boat or aircraft occasionally sank a ship filled with arms. Consequently, tensions between the United States and Germany grew

Japan, which was ruled by a dictator, had become a member of the Germany-Italy axis in 1940. Primarily because of Japan's war with China, the United States placed an embargo on materials that were to be shipped to Japan. Of course, citizens of the United States sympathized with the Chinese, not necessarily the Japanese. Although talks between leaders of the United States and Japan lasted months, the invasion of Russia by Germany turned each country's attention toward Europe. Further talks continued when Japan invaded Indochina. Before the United States resumed sending materials, the United States demanded that Japan withdraw from Indochina and not invade the Dutch East Indies. Discussions continued. However, neither country would compromise on China. On December 7, 1941, the Japanese bombed the naval installation of the United States at Pearl Harbor, which caused President Roosevelt to ask Congress for a declaration of war against Japan. When Germany and Italy declared war against the United States three days later, the United States reciprocated.

The United States was at a disadvantage in the sense that she had to support her allies and herself. Nonetheless, she succeeded in playing a major role in the war. Indeed, without her help, the Allied Nations, including Great Britain, more than likely would have lost. Although the war—any war—was expensive, it had a positive effect on the United States: it actually brought the country out of the Great Depression, which had lasted years. Men were drafted for military service and women increased their families' income by obtaining positions in various factories. Military innovations were rapidly developed and deployed. The farmer who had been plagued with misfortune during the 1930s benefited as prices of agricultural products more than doubled.

The war failed to benefit everyone, however. Although African-Americans were employed, Japanese-Americans, if they did not serve in the military, were moved to concentration camps.

Like previous wars, in order to purchase necessary munitions such as aircraft, ships, tanks, and firearms, among other goods, the federal government had to spend. As a result, more than $300 billion left the federal government. By the time the war ended, the national debt had increased to $258.7 billion.

President Roosevelt became involved in the war as his decisions and subsequent policies effected both sides of the Atlantic Ocean. He authorized the development of the atomic bomb. He traveled to war zones and to conferences, where heads of states planned strategies and even postwar policies.

In 1944 President Roosevelt was severely criticized by leading members of Congress and leading members of associations and organizations. Nonetheless, even though he suffered from poor health, he defeated Thomas E. Dewey. He traveled to the Conference at Yalta, in the Russian Crimea, to discuss the aims of the United States, Great Britain, and Russia after the war ended. When he returned to the United States, he traveled to Warm Springs, Georgia, where he rested. Unfortunately, he died in April 1945, just before Germany's armed forces collapsed. Harry S. Truman, his new vice-president, became president.

Contrary to popular opinion, except for providing temporary jobs to unemployed people and offering hope, only a few of the New Deal programs had any major impact on the every day person during the Great Depression. For instance, when President Roosevelt entered the White

House, the unemployment figure was 24.9 percent. In 1940 the unemployment figure was 14.6 percent. Although unemployment had improved, it was still a major problem. However, as the United States prepared for World War II in 1941, the unemployment figure dropped to 9.9 percent. This figure dropped considerably each year thereafter. For instance, in 1945 the unemployment figure was 1.9 percent. In essence, World War II created more jobs than all of the New Deal programs together.

A few of the New Deal programs have had some positive effect. For instance, Social Security has helped many people, particularly the elderly. Unfortunately, as mentioned, Congress has added to this act over the years; consequently, it has become too costly for the country's own good because it offers too many programs to too many people. In other words, Social Security was actually intended for those who had paid into it. Now, it covers individuals who have not paid into it. Of course, there are a few other programs, including the act pertaining to banking, which protects depositors, and the act pertaining to labor, which protects workers.

Harry S. Truman had been born in Missouri and had grown up on a farm. He had worked in a bank and as a farmer. He had served as an officer in the United States Army during World War I. After having managed a haberdashery store and after attending the Kansas City Law School in Kansas City, he had served as a judge in Missouri.

In 1934 he had been elected to the United States Senate and had supported President Roosevelt's New Deal programs. Ten years later he had been nominated as President Roosevelt's vice-president.

As president, Truman immediately wanted to end the war. Germany, its armed forces depleted, surrendered. In order to bring an end to the war in Japan, Truman authorized the dropping of an atomic bomb on Hiroshima and, later, another on Nagasaki, in Japan. Japan surrendered soon after.

Although Truman learned quickly, he was unaware of many of the minute problems facing the United States. For instance, the pledge made by the Russians at the Yalta Conference were, for the most part, broken. When he met with Joseph Stalin and Churchill at Potsdam,

Germany, the Russian leader failed to satisfy his requests. Stalin was merely looking after his own interests as were the United States and Great Britain. Since Stalin had broken his pledges by enlarging Russia's western border, tensions between the countries increased. The Cold War was under way.

The United States began demobilizing her military forces. Since she had the atomic bomb, a sense of security was present. Abroad, however, Russia was aiding Communists in Greece and Turkey. Great Britain, which had been providing aid to counter the Communists, was suffering. She could no longer afford such aid. Truman immediately asked Congress to appropriate funds for aid for the two countries. This request became known as the Truman Doctrine. Within two years, by 1949, Communist aggression was no longer a threat to either country.

Although the United States proposed through the United Nations—an organization that had been promoted by President Roosevelt in 1944 but had failed to materialize until after his death—a plan to control atomic energy, Russia refused to agree unless the United States destroyed her nuclear arsenal. Of course, the United States refused. Through the Atomic Energy Commission, which had been established by the Atomic Energy Act of 1946, further research into atomic power was conducted. However, Russia pursued the same goal. As a result, the Cold War intensified.

Truman and the Congress reorganized the military structure basically for the purpose of unification. In 1947 the National Security Act was passed. The act created the National Security Council and a cabinet position—the Secretary of Defense. It enabled the United States Air Force to become a separate military service. Two years later the Department of Defense was established to further unification.

In 1947 Secretary of State George C. Marshall proposed that the European countries develop a plan for European recovery. Within weeks representatives from European nations met in Paris, France. The eventual plan, which became known as the Marshall Plan, was sound in the sense that the United States could not afford to feed the impoverished people of Europe forever. Russia pulled out, denouncing the plan as American imperialism. Representatives from Russia's satellite countries, Finland

and Czechoslovakia, were intimidated and subsequently stayed away from the conference. Representatives from 16 other European nations remained and participated in the Committee of European Economic Cooperation. The committee planned to have Europe reconstructed by 1951. The United States Congress established in 1948 the Economic Cooperation Administration (ECA) when Czech Communists assumed power in Prague. The United States supported Europe's efforts by spending $12 billion through the ECA.

In 1948 the Soviet Union attempted to blockade routes in Germany to slow down the European efforts, especially in Berlin. The western nations retaliated and flew in supplies, and the Soviet Union ended its blockade. The blockade, which lasted 11 months, persuaded many European leaders and President Truman that only an alliance could dissuade the Soviet Union from further action. The North Atlantic Treaty Organization (NATO), which was signed by 12 nations in 1949 and which defended part of Europe from the Soviet Union, was the result.

Although Truman had asked Congress for a 21-point domestic program that called for new wages and working hours, an expanded social security program, new public-housing legislation, and a Fair Employment Practices Act, among others, Congress failed to fulfill his request. Of course, Congress had other problems to consider, such as military demobilization and its impact on the economy. Re-conversion, though a major problem, was merely one that members of Congress faced. The Communist threat abroad as well as at home was another. Nonetheless, re-conversion seemed the easier one to solve. Members of the military received benefits, war contracts were cancelled, bureaucratic agencies were curtailed, and unwanted or unneeded factories were sold.

The people of the United States had unlimited buying power or credit, but few goods were available. Consequently, prices increased. Strikes were the result. Unions, which had been controlled during the war, were free to strike for increased wages. Leaders of businesses and farmers attempted to end price controls on products and agricultural commodities. However, Congress enacted a new price-control bill. Truman, who had been in favor of the controls, reversed his decision on most of them when he realized that it was to his political advantage. It should be pointed out that conservative Republicans were elected in 1948 to both the House of Representatives and the Senate of the United States. President Truman had to struggle to get appropriate legislation passed. For instance, the Labor Management Relations Act, which was the Taft-Hartley Act, placed additional restrictions on organized labor, had been vetoed by Truman, but overridden by Congress in 1947. In 1948, again over President Truman's veto, Congress passed additional bills, including a tax bill that reduced the taxes of the wealthy by as much as 60 percent (individual income tax rates ranged from 20 percent to 91 percent at the time). Over the years members of Congress had increased taxes and had created a cash cow. Seldom did any member think about lowering the rates.

Although Truman's supporters helped him defeat Republican Thomas E. Dewey, States' Rights (Dixiecrat) Governor J. Strom Thurmond, and Progressive Vice-President Henry A. Wallace in 1948, his political philosophy had caused the Democratic Party to splinter into several anti-Truman groups. His Fair Deal legislation for federal aid to education, health insurance, and civil rights was, for the most part, overlooked by Congress. In fact, his proposal for civil rights was opposed by many members of Congress.

Within the federal government, employees, especially those who worked in the Department of State, were found to be Communists or Communist sympathizers and subsequently dismissed or, in some cases, charged. In 1950 the McCarran Internal Security Act, which restricted activities by Communists within the nation, was passed. The same year, Alger Hiss, a Department of State employee, was convicted of perjury. In 1951 Julius and Ethel Rosenberg, who had provided secret documents to the Soviet Union, were convicted of being spies for the Communists and subsequently executed. Senator Joseph McCarthy, who never provided proof other than waving sheets of paper, claimed that he knew the names of numerous Department of State employees who were Communists. The papers he waved supposedly contained the names of these employees. In addition, scandal infiltrated the White House. It was learned later that certain employees under President Truman had received bribes for various activities. As if these questionable and unscrupulous individuals and their activities were not grave enough, the Korean War may have been worse.

The Korean War had started in 1950, when the North Koreans moved below the 38th parallel. President Truman, acting responsibly, brought the subject before the Security Council of the United Nations, which first passed a resolution demanding that the North Koreans move behind the 38th parallel and later asked the United Nations to support the Republic of Korea. Truman sent aid to the South Koreans, and, later, at the request of the United Nations, dispatched American armed forces as well as armed forces from other nations that were members of the United Nations to support South Korea. War resulted. Under General Douglas MacArthur, the forces of the United Nations moved to the 38th parallel and beyond. Unfortunately, Communist China intervened. The forces of the United Nations were driven below the 38th parallel. General MacArthur wished for a full-scale war, but President Truman denied him his wish. Instead, Truman ordered MacArthur to return to the United States. General Matthew Ridgway took command and eventually captured Seoul and crossed the 38th parallel. When President Truman fired General MacArthur, Truman's popularity, which had been slowly decreasing every month since the late 1940s, dropped dramatically. General MacArthur was a military hero to the people of the United States. Truman was just another politician.

Of course, primarily for the war in Korea, President Truman had requested Congress to increase the military budget, which had not been popular. After all, the federal government had spent large amounts during World War II. Besides, the people of the United States were not ready for another war, especially a war in Asia. In fact, they were repulsed by the thought of war.

President Truman did not seek another term in 1952. Instead, he supported Democratic Governor Adlai Stevenson of Illinois who ran against Republican Dwight David Eisenhower, the former military hero who had been responsible for leading the Allied Forces in Europe during World War II. Eisenhower easily defeated Stevenson.

After the election, Truman retired to Missouri and wrote his memoirs. He spoke about national affairs from time to time. He had been criticized for several decisions while serving as president, but years later many leaders changed their minds about his presidency.

Eisenhower had been born in Texas and had grown up on a small farm in Kansas. In 1911 he had entered the United States Military Academy at West Point, New York, where he had been a notable athlete.

Eisenhower had married Mamie Doud in 1916 and had two sons, one of whom had died as a child. Eisenhower had served in the United States Army during World War I and had become a brigadier general when World War II started. In 1943, when he had become a full general, he had been the Supreme Commander of the Allied Forces in Europe.

He had resigned from the United States Army in 1948 to become the president of Columbia University. Later, former President Truman had requested that he return to Europe to command NATO's armed forces, which he did.

As president, Eisenhower listened to his advisors, several of whom were former leaders of businesses and industries. He did not believe that the federal government should interfere as much as it had in the nation's economy.

In 1953 the Korean War, which had taken thousands of lives, ended in a stalemate. Finally, the war was over. Unfortunately, the weak peace that had been obtained may have allowed Communism to spread. Of course, John Foster Dulles, who was the secretary of state at the time, may have been naïve in his thinking. After all, the United States had the atomic bomb. What Communist countries would be crazy enough to be aggressive? This thought, perhaps more than any other, may have crossed the secretary of state's mind. It may have played a role in how Eisenhower dealt with Communism. His use of the Central Intelligence Agency (CIA) to counter Communism and intervene in countries' affairs, though several political figures advised him against this, was reckless in the sense that the repercussions were undeniably great. The respect that countries had for the United States dwindled somewhat as a result. Eisenhower was warned at the time, but he failed to halt the CIA's clandestine activities.

Eisenhower made several commitments abroad. Indeed, Dulles organized the Southeast Asia Treaty Organization (SEATO), which brought together three Asian countries—Thailand, Pakistan, and the Philippines—and the United States, Australia, Britain, France, and New Zealand, and, later, Cambodia, Laos, and South Vietnam. He encouraged Britain to create the Central Treaty Organization (CENTO) for the Middle East.

President Eisenhower's foreign policy, which included the Atoms for Peace Plan of 1953 as well as proposals for controlling atomic arsenals, influenced leaders to use nuclear science not only for military weapons but for the world's welfare. .

A year later Senator Joseph McCarthy of Wisconsin, who had claimed he had lists of known Communists who worked for the federal government, now claimed Communists were in the military and working at the Pentagon. Although Eisenhower had strongly disapproved of McCarthy's previous allegations, he had not made any public statements regarding them. Now that McCarthy had made comments about employees at the Pentagon, Eisenhower followed the United States Army investigation of the senator's outrageous comments. During the Army-McCarthy hearings, the lawyer representing the Army basically exposed McCarthy for what he was, a charlatan who would stoop to any level to get publicity. However, there were Communist sympathizers who had worked for the federal government, especially in the 1930s and 1940s.[5] Many of these employees were rooted out over the years. Several were determined to be spies for the Soviet Union and were imprisoned or executed.

President Eisenhower balanced the budget in the mid-1950s. He attempted to decrease federal spending and subsequently limit the federal government's role in society. He encouraged the federal government to allow so-called federal projects (such as the construction of dams) be built by private enterprises. His policies, which were the opposite of former President Truman's and former President Roosevelt's, gained the support of Democratic members of Congress.

In 1955 Eisenhower suffered a heart attack. Although months passed before he recuperated, he announced in 1956 that he would accept the nomination for reelection. The Democrats nominated Adlai Stevenson. Before the election, problems abroad occurred. These included the Soviet Communist Party in Poland, the Soviet Union's army in Hungary, Israel's dispute with Egypt over its border, and the Britain and France attack on Egypt over the control of the Suez Canal. Although these problems stirred the emotions of American voters, Eisenhower, primarily because of his popularity, easily defeated Stevenson.

President Eisenhower's second term was filled with domestic issues, including an economic recession that caused high unemployment and labor disputes, as well as a scandal that forced several political and one military figure to resign.

In 1956 Eisenhower signed the Interstate Highway Act, which funded 90 percent of the construction costs on a new, four-lane interstate highway system. Eventually, this system was named for him. Although he cut budgets for public housing, he encouraged Congress to support scientific education.

Eisenhower promised to uphold the laws of the nation, including the ruling by the United States Supreme Court regarding segregation in public schools. For instance, in 1957 the governor of Arkansas posted armed men outside Little Rock Central High School to prevent African-American children from entering. This action was covered by the press. When a federal district court ordered the governor to allow the children into the school, he did, but he provided little protection for the children. Eisenhower reacted by sending federal troops to protect the rights of the children.

The same year he approved of the United States Commission on Civil Rights. He also encouraged leading members of Congress to pass measures that focused on the economy, especially measures for stimulating businesses and industries, which had experienced decreases in production and in wages. The measures included lowering taxes, lowering credit rates, expanding coverage by Social Security, and building highways. In addition, he increased spending for defense and sent aid to other countries.

When the Soviet Union sent Sputnik, a satellite, into space, Eisenhower and leading members of Congress grew alarmed. As a result, Congress passed and Eisenhower signed the National Aeronautics and

Space Act, which established the National Aeronautics and Space Administration in 1958.

The same year he sent the United States Marines to Lebanon primarily to prevent possible Communist aggression. However, the United States could do little in other countries, particularly in those that had corrupt presidents or leaders and administrations. In some cases, these presidents or leaders were worse than Communist leaders when it came to helping their respective peoples. Consequently, it came as no surprise when Communism spread to Vietnam and Latin America. Dictatorships only forced people to retaliate. When Stalin had died in 1953, certain American diplomats thought the Soviet Union's aggressive policies would be relaxed. Just the opposite had occurred. Eisenhower supported the South Vietnamese in its efforts against Communism, but he was opposed to sending a large military unit to the country. In short, he opposed war, including a so-called limited war. He believed that the security of freedom throughout the world depended on the health and strength of the United States, especially its economy. Of course, the United States economy could be destroyed by the federal government becoming too large and spending needlessly. Consequently, he was opposed to reckless spending.

In 1959 he met with the leader of the Soviet Union, Nikita Khrushchev, at Camp David, in Pennsylvania. In 1960 he met with him again at the summit meeting in Paris, France, primarily to improve relations between the two powers. Unfortunately, one of the CIA's spy aircraft, the U-2, had been shot down over the Soviet Union. The pilot, Captain Gary Powers, was captured alive, and Khrushchev demanded that President Eisenhower reprimand those responsible and cease further missions. Eisenhower refused. The summit meeting ended. Perhaps the incident accelerated the Soviet Union's mission.

Before he left the White House, President Eisenhower advised his successor about Southeast Asia and Cuba, and what he would do if he were president. He also warned the nation about the "military-industrial complex" in his last presidential address. He said this combination of interests could be disastrous for "our liberties or democratic processes."

Primarily because of President Eisenhower's beliefs, guidance, maturation, and military experience, the 1950s was one of the most prosperous and secure decades in the nation's history. However, his efforts to reduce the size of the federal government were in vain. When he left office, the size had not been reduced.

After Eisenhower left the White House, a few presidents who followed him sought his advice. He died in 1969 from a heart attack.

* * *

The social climate from 1901 to 1961 changed with each presidential election. At the turn of the century, many Americans were poor, uneducated, overworked, and living in slums. The wealthy existed, but in most cases they had obtained their wealth at the expense of others. Inequities abounded. Thus organized labor achieved strength by making demands on employers. American women who were employed in various industries, but particularly the garment industry, achieved unionization. In addition, they fought for prohibition. Farm organizations flourished. Socialistic organizations as well as publications appeared. Journalists, especially the muckrakers—a term that had been applied to investigative journalists by President Theodore Roosevelt, informed the citizenry about the opening of the West, the various problems confronting cities, and the unscrupulous practices by managers and owners of large companies, especially monopolies. The muckrakers wrote extensive articles and books that stirred the emotions of their readers. Of course, several of these investigative journalists had personal vendettas against the subjects about which they wrote. Criticism also came from intellectuals such as Oliver Wendell Holmes, Jr., John Dewey, and Thorstein Veblen.

The Progressive Movement was prevalent in the United States. New forms of government appeared in various cities and states. The aldermanic system was replaced with either a commission or city manager form of government in city after city, primarily because of corruption. Thus progressivism spread from the cities to the states and eventually to the White House.

When World War I occurred, Americans were concerned with the United States, not Europe. Visions of an idealistic nation were common. After all, the United States had progressed economically and spiritually. However, when men were called for military service, they proved that the United States was not only a strong country, but a country that enjoyed victory. When they returned home, they witnessed labor strikes, racial prejudice, various Communist parties, bombings in Washington, D. C., and anarchy.

Progress returned in the early 1920s, when business practices changed. Assembly line automation was common; wages increased as production increased. Nonetheless, the majority of Americans remained fixed in their prejudices. They disliked people from abroad, especially when they were willing to work for less. Some white, Anglo-Saxon protestants deemed themselves superior to African-Americans and other races. In the South, members of the Ku Klux Klan intimidated and even murdered those they opposed. Although the terrorist organization grew in size in the early 1920s, its power grew weaker when certain journalists and a Klansman exposed the corruption within the organization and its ties to certain political figures.

The 1920s saw the emergence of organized crime, particularly in Chicago. Al Capone became an enemy of the United States government, but not until he had amassed a fortune from illegal means, such as gambling and prostitution, and had ordered the deaths of more than a hundred competing gangsters.

On the lighter side, Americans enjoyed various forms of music, movies, radio, vaudeville, bootlegged liquor, dancing, and, of course, the automobile. Realistic novels and tabloid newspapers filled with sensational stories and photographs entertained them for hours. Sports, particularly baseball, grew in popularity. The Jazz Age alienated some and enlightened others.

In 1929 the years of prosperity came to an end for millions of Americans. The Great Depression gripped the country for much of the next decade. In such a climate of rampant unemployment, violence was not unheard of; indeed, disputes between the veterans of World War I and the federal government, and between farmers and officials occurred more than once. Although Roosevelt put fears of many Americans to rest, there were those who failed to believe what he said during his many "fireside chats." His legislation, although it failed to help every unemployed American find work, did restore the American spirit by providing aid. For instance, electricity was provided for the first time to many rural and farming areas. Organized labor emerged as a force with which manufacturers had to deal. African-Americans as well as Indians were recognized as citizens and subsequently provided with assistance.

Before America fully recovered, however, World War II began in Europe. Americans, for the most part, were isolationists; they did not desire to fight. Japan, perhaps provoked by American diplomacy, bombed Pearl Harbor, and Americans were eager to fight. As American men were called to serve in the armed forces, American women obtained employment on a grand scale. The war effort was important. When the war ended, many women remained in various positions, even though the government tried to persuade them to return to their homes so that their loved ones could return to work.

Before the Korean War started in 1950, Americans were once again experiencing prosperity. Many married couples were working. Purchasing power per family increased just in time to buy a new invention called television. Audiences became fascinated by westerns, comedies, and children's programs.

Concurrently, the rebirth of the red scare emerged and story after story filled newspapers and influenced the beliefs of Americans. By the time the Korean War ended, the red scare had catapulted two senators—Senator Richard M. Nixon and Senator Joseph McCarthy—to unwarranted attention. Millions of Americans watched on television the Army-McCarthy hearings in which Senator McCarthy claimed that Communist spies had infiltrated the military. Fortunately, the red scare became a minor fear when the United States Senate finally censured McCarthy in 1954.

During the 1950s, certain African-Americans, such as Dr. Martin Luther King, led black marches and boycotts for the purpose of civil rights. Eventually, these African-American leaders gained support and legislation was enacted to guarantee African-Americans civil rights, including the right to attend public schools of their choice and to vote.

Throughout much of the 1950s Americans enjoyed job security. The young, the first television generation, merely sought more of what their parents had. Conservatism seemed to have spread from the government to the state to the city to the corporation to the individual. Indeed, conservatism was pervasive and intrusive in every aspect of society. As a result, the nation prospered.

Another side to this complacency existed in the so-called "beat generation," or young people who rebelled. However, their emergence was dissimilar to the nonconformists of the 1920s in the sense they had few ideas to promote. Nor were they like the multitudes of the 1960s, that rebelled because of their ideas or because to do so was popular. Although they admired certain actors, writers, and musicians, the music of Elvis Presley and other rock and roll artists failed to hold their attention because the music was accepted by too many people.

Notes:

1. Ever since the federal income tax was enacted, the national debt has increased substantially, perhaps leading one to believe that presidents have not been *that* concerned about cutting spending. After all, as a result of a federal income tax, the federal government takes in a vast amount of money every week, month, and year.

The federal income tax may be the primary reason certain succeeding presidents have enacted legislation that have expanded the role of the federal government. They know more and more money will be taken in by the federal government. Remember, each bureaucratic entity created by the federal government requires money to function. The question is whether each bureaucratic entity is necessary. Furthermore, depending on what the bureaucratic entity's function is, one's freedom may be restricted as a result, which is certainly not what the founders had in mind.

2. Joseph A. Schumpeter, "Depressions," in *The Economics of the Recovery Program* by Douglass V. Brown, et al. (New York: Whittlesey House, McGraw-Hill, 1934), 20.
3. Paul A. Samuelson and William D Nordhaus, *Economics*, 12 ed. (New York: McGraw-Hill, 1985), 389.
4. Arthur M. Schlesinger, Jr., *The Age of Roosevelt: The Coming of the New Deal* (Vol. 2) (Boston: Houghton Mifflin, 1958), 311-312.
5. George F. Kennan, *Memoirs: 1925-50.* (Boston: Little, Brown and Co., 1957), 191-2.

References:

Allen, Frederick Lewis. *The Big Change: America Transforms Itself: 1900-1950*. New York: Harper & Row, 1952.

Ambrose, Stephen E. *Eisenhower the President*. New York: Simon & Schuster, 1984.

Ambrose, Stephen E. *Eisenhower: Soldier and President*. Hartford, CT: American Political Biography Press, 2007.

Baker, Ray Stannard. *Woodrow Wilson: Life and Letters* (7 vols.). New York: Charles Scribner's Sons, 1946.

Berg, A. Scott. *Wilson*. New York: G. P. Putnam's Sons, 2013.

Blum, John M. *The Progressive Presidents: Roosevelt, Wilson, Roosevelt, Johnson*. New York: W. W. Norton, 1980.

Brands, H. W. *Traitor to His Class: The Privileged Life and Radical Presidency of Franklin Delano Roosevelt*. New York: Doubleday, 2006.

Burner, David. *Herbert Hoover: A Public Life*. New York: Knopf, 1979.

Burns, James McGregor. *The American Experiment: The Crosswinds of Freedom*. New York: Knopf, 1989.

Caute, David. *The Great Fear: The Anti-Communist Purge Under Truman and Eisenhower*. New York: Simon & Schuster, 1978.

Chalmers, David M. *Hooded Americanism: The First Century of the Ku Klux Klan, 1865-1965*. New York: Doubleday, 1965.

Chernow, Ron. *Titan: The Life of John D. Rockefeller*. New York: Random House, 1998.

Coletta, Paola E. *The Presidency of William Howard Taft*. Lawrence: University Press of Kansas, 1973.

Collier, Peter and David Horowitz. *The Roosevelts: An American Saga*. New York: Simon & Schuster, 1994.

Conkin, Paul K. *FDR and the Origins of the Welfare State*. New York: Crowell, 1967.

Davis, Kenneth S. *FDR: The New Deal Years, 1933-1937*. New York: Random House, 1986.

Dean, John W. *Warren G. Harding*. New York: Times Books, 2004.

Downes, Randolph C. *The Rise of Warren Gambiel Harding, 1865-1920*. Columbus, Ohio: Ohio State University Press, 1970.

Fausold, Martin L. *The Presidency of Herbert Hoover*. Lawrence: University Press of Kansas, 1985.

Ferrell, Robert H. *Harry S. Truman: A Life*. Hartford, CT: American Political Biography Press, 2007.

Flood, Charles Bracelen. *Hitler: The Path to Power*. Boston: Houghton Mifflin, 1989.

Galbraith, John Kenneth. *The Great Crash: 1929*. Boston: Houghton Mifflin, 1972.

Garrison, Elisha E. *Roosevelt, Wilson and the Federal Reserve Law*. Boston: Christopher Publishing House, 1931.

Gould, Lewis L. *The Presidency of Theodore Roosevelt*. Lawrence: University Press of Kansas, 1991.

Gould, Lewis L. *The William Howard Taft Presidency*. Lawrence: University Press of Kansas, 2009.

Hamby, Alonzo L. *Man of the People: a Life of Harry S. Truman*. New York: Oxford University Press, 1995.

Harbaugh, William Henry. *Power and Responsibility: Theodore Roosevelt*. Hartford, CT: American Political Biography Press, 1997.

Heckscher, August. *Woodrow Wilson: A Biography*. New York: Charles Scribner's Sons, 1991.

Hughes, Emmet John. *The Ordeal of Power: a Political Memoir of the Eisenhower Years*. New York: Atheneum, 1963.

Keegan, John. *The First World War*. New York: Knopf, 1999.

Lash, Joseph P. *Eleanor and Franklin*. New York: W. W. Norton, 1971.

Link, Arthur S. *Wilson* (5 vols.). Princeton, N.J.: Princeton University Press, 1947-65.

Lodge, Henry Cabot. *The Senate and the League of Nations*. New York: Charles Scribner's Sons, 1925.

Lyons, Eugene. *Herbert Hoover: A Biography*. Norwalk, CT: The Easton Press, 1965.

Manchester, William. *The Glory and the Dream: A Narrative History of America 1932-72*. Boston: Little, Brown, 1974.

McCoy, Donald R. *Calvin Coolidge: The Quiet President*. New York: Macmillan, 1967.

McCullough, David. *Truman*. New York: Simon & Schuster, 1992.

McElvaine, Robert S. *The Great Depression: America, 1929-1941*. New York: Times Books, 1993.

Morgan, Ted. *FDR: A Biography*. New York: Simon & Schuster, 1985.

Morris, Edmund. *Colonel Roosevelt*. New York: Random House Trade Paperbacks, 2011.

Morris, Edmund. *The Rise of Theodore Roosevelt*. New York: Random House Trade Paperbacks, 2001.

Morris, Edmund. *Theodore Rex*. New York: Random House, 2001.

Mowry, George E. *Theodore Roosevelt and the Progressive Movement*. Madison: University of Wisconsin Press, 1946.

Murray, Robert. *The Harding Era: Warren G. Harding and His Administration*. Minneapolis: University of Minnesota Press, 1969.

Nash, George H. *The Life of Herbert Hoover* (2 vols.). New York: W. W. Norton, 1983-8.

Newton, Jim. *Eisenhower: The White House Years*. New York: Doubleday, 2011.

Pringle, Henry F. *The Life and Times of William Howard Taft: A Biography* (2 vols.). Norwalk, CT: Easton Press, 1986.

Rappleye, Charles. *Herbert Hoover in the White House: The Ordeal of the Presidency*. New York: Simon & Schuster, 2016.

Schwartz, Jordan A. *The New Dealers: Power Politics in the Age of Roosevelt*. New York: Knopf, 1993.

Shlaes, Amity. *Coolidge*. New York: Harper, 2013.

Smith, Jean Edward. *Eisenhower in War and Peace*. New York: Random House, 2012.

Smith, Jean Edward. *FDR*. New York: Random House, 2007.

Sobel, Robert. *Coolidge, An American Enigma*. Washington, D. C.: Regnery, 2000.

Thompson, John A. *Reformers and War: American Progressive Publicists and the First World War*. New York: Cambridge University Press, 1987.

Toland, John. *Adolf Hitler*. Garden City, N. Y.: Doubleday, 1976.

Walworth, Arthur. *Woodrow Wilson: American Prophet* (Vol. 1). Norwalk, CT: The Easton Press, 1978.

Walworth, Arthur. *Woodrow Wilson: World Prophet* (Vol. 2). Norwalk, CT: The Easton Press, 1978.

Wilson, Joan Hoff. *Herbert Hoover: Forgotten Progressive*. Boston: Little, Brown, 1975.

Chapter 5

Political and Social Change in the United States from 1961 to 2000

John Fitzgerald Kennedy had been born in Massachusetts. His father, Joseph Kennedy, had served as chairman of the Securities and Exchange Commission and as ambassador to Great Britain during the administration of President Franklin Delano Roosevelt.

John Kennedy had studied at the London School of Economics and had graduated from Harvard University in 1940. He had served in the United States Navy during World War II. In fact, he had saved at least one crewman of PT 109, a patrol boat, in 1943.

After the war, in 1946, Kennedy had been elected to the United States House of Representatives. In 1952 he had been elected to the United States Senate. In 1953 he had married Jacqueline (Jackie) Bouvier. His book, *Profiles in Courage*, which concerned several politicians who had adhered to their beliefs, had been improved by other writers and editors before it had been published in 1956.

In 1960, at the Democratic National Convention, Kennedy had been nominated for president. Later, he had debated Vice President Richard M. Nixon, the popular Republican candidate for the presidency. The debates had been televised, and Kennedy had captivated the viewing audience with his youth, charm, and intellect. Without question, the television image of Kennedy had been more appealing than the television image of Nixon. In fact, certain critics believed that the debates had contributed greatly to Nixon's defeat. Television, which had entertained millions of Americans during Nixon's terms as vice president, had depicted a tired, haggard man. People who had watched the debates on television had not been made aware that Nixon had been ill before the debates.

Kennedy had won the election by a narrow margin. In fact, there had been questions about certain ballots in Illinois and Texas. In Illinois, for instance, it had been alleged that ballots had been cast by people who had died.

As president, Kennedy initiated the Peace Corps, which Congress approved, in 1961. The Peace Corps appealed to young men and women in the United States who were interested in helping those who lived in underdeveloped countries. The Peace Corps also displayed the benevolence of the United States.

Perhaps Kennedy's greatest contribution to the United States was his views on space exploration. When the Soviet Union put a man in space in 1961, the United States, he realized, had to meet another challenge. Consequently, his positive efforts encouraged Congress to meet the challenge. Later the same year the United States succeeded in sending a man into space.

When Fidel Castro, a Communist, became the dictator of Cuba after Fulgencio Battista fled in 1959, the United States had been reluctant to do anything about it. President Eisenhower had entertained several military plans, but had failed to attempt any invasion that would have removed Castro from power.

Unlike President Eisenhower, Kennedy approved an invasion of Cuba by primarily Cuban refugees in 1961. These refugees were helped by the Central Intelligence Agency (CIA). However, the invasion at the Bahia de Cochinas (Bay of Pigs) was a disaster primarily because Castro had been made aware of the invasion, and Kennedy had been too weak and indecisive to see the mission through. Castro's armed forces killed and captured more than 1,000 men. President Kennedy did not have the resolve to provide naval and air support. Consequently, even though the United States had ships and aircraft in the area, they did not fire on Castro's men or offer support to the refugees. Of course, press coverage was not positive, and President Kennedy was humiliated.

In 1962 aerial surveillance revealed that the Soviet Union had started building missile sites in Cuba. In addition, Soviet ships had delivered medium-range missiles to the island country. Kennedy was informed and ordered a blockade primarily to prevent additional Soviet ships from entering Cuba. After a lengthy standoff between Kennedy and the leader of the Soviet Union, Nikita Khrushchev, the two came to an agreement. Khrushchev would withdraw the missiles from Cuba if Kennedy would promise not to invade the island. Kennedy agreed. The missiles were removed. Later, Kennedy withdrew missiles from Turkey.

Instead of invading Cuba and ousting the Soviet Union's troops and missiles from the island, Kennedy had agreed to Khrushchev's demands, which may have been what the leader had wanted all along. As a result, Castro continued as the dictator of Cuba, periodically sending military forces to various parts of the world, including Africa, Asia, Central America, and South America.

On a different front, Kennedy promised that the United States would continue to support West Germany. However, he was confronted with another major problem, which was Vietnam. South Vietnam was under Premier Ngo Dinh Diem and his brother, Ngo Dinh Nhu. Both had failed to have a government that certain groups expected. Although Kennedy disagreed with Diem's policies, he ordered "advisers" into the country to help train the South Vietnamese Army, which at the time outnumbered the Viet Cong ten-fold. On the advice of Vice-President Lyndon Johnson and others, Kennedy increased the number of "advisers." These men eventually saw combat. Premier Ngo Dinh Diem was assassinated in 1963. It should be mentioned that Kennedy was not necessarily interested in escalating the war in Vietnam. In fact, if he thought the South Vietnamese could not win the war, more than likely he would have halted American involvement altogether.

In Washington, D. C., Jackie Kennedy brought glamour to the White House. She was more attractive and much younger compared to other First Ladies who had lived there. Eventually, she changed the interior of the residence and afterward conducted a tour of the White House that was televised so viewers could see the changes.

Kennedy, a Roman Catholic, proposed domestic policies that he called the New Frontier, which was similar to what presidents Franklin Roosevelt and Harry Truman had proposed in the sense that it called for immediate action by Congress to initiate legislation for a stronger national defense, additional foreign aid, health care for the elderly, greater conservation, aid to education, greater housing as well as community development, and additional funding for highway construction. However, Kennedy was reluctant to combat Congress over most of his domestic policies. Consequently, only a few bills that increased the minimum wage, improved transit systems, middle-income housing in cities, and retrained the unemployed were approved. The latter was in reaction to what was happening primarily in the South. Whenever African-Americans marched or demonstrated for equal rights, numerous combating whites confronted them. Even the so-called "Freedom Riders" who traveled to the South to peacefully demonstrate were attacked. When Dr. Martin Luther King, Jr., inspired hundreds of other African-Americans to peacefully demonstrate, these groups were attacked as well. Such confrontations brought attention to a major problem in the United States.

Kennedy's policies encouraged developing Third World countries to seek independence and economic prosperity through democratic means. Unfortunately, such programs as the Peace Corps failed to counter Soviet aggression.

In 1963, after the leaders of nuclear-armed countries realized that nuclear war should never occur, a nuclear test-ban treaty was signed. Representatives from the United States, Great Britain, and the Soviet Union agreed to stop further testing of nuclear weapons in outer space, in the atmosphere, and under water. Only underground tests could be conducted. Although France and China refused to sign, within weeks other nations agreed to the treaty.

Unfortunately, on November 22, 1963, Kennedy was assassinated while riding in an opened presidential limousine in Dallas, Texas. Although several individuals claimed they had seen shots fired from more than one location, the Warren Commission, which was chaired by Chief Justice Earl Warren of the United States Supreme Court, determined that Lee Harvey Oswald, a former United States Marine who had lived and worked in the Soviet Union, had been the lone gunman.

Kennedy became more popular among the public after his death. Vice President Lyndon Baines Johnson became president.

Johnson had been born in Texas and had graduated from Southwest Texas State Teachers College (now Texas State University). He had taught high school and had married Claudia "Lady Bird" Taylor before he had been elected to the House of Representatives of the United States in 1936. He had run for the United States Senate in 1941, but he had lost. However, in 1948, he had run for the Senate and had won.

Having served in both houses of Congress, Johnson had wanted the Democrats to nominate him for president in 1960, but they had nominated John F. Kennedy instead. They had nominated him for vice president, which he had accepted.

When Kennedy was shot and killed, Johnson became president. Although Johnson did not have the charisma of Kennedy, he certainly exhibited more power than his predecessor probably because he had been Senate majority leader. In addition, he knew the important power brokers of both houses. Without question, he achieved more domestically speaking than Kennedy had. However, his intentional escalation of the war in Vietnam was his downfall.

As president, Johnson supported the former president's domestic programs, including legislation concerning civil rights and taxes. Immediately, he encouraged Congress to pass the Civil Rights Act, which had been presented before Kennedy was killed. This act, which had been developed in reaction to the inequality that African-Americans, especially those who lived in the South, experienced, was passed. In fact, the inequality was so prevalent in parts of the South that African-Americans had to demonstrate to have their voices heard.

He persuaded Congress to pass the tax-reduction bill that Kennedy had proposed, which it did. In 1964 the Economic Opportunity Act, which tackled depressed areas in cities by encouraging economic development through Job Corps, Neighborhood Youth Corps, Volunteers in Service to America (VISTA), and Community Action, was signed into law.

President Johnson was undeniably for the poor, the African-American, and other minority groups, including the aged. Therefore, it was no surprise when he and former senator, Hubert Humphrey, of Minnesota won the election in 1964. Johnson's opponent, Senator Barry

Goldwater of Arizona, a conservative Republican, failed to persuade voters that he was the right man for president. Of course, the famous "Daisy" commercial, which had been created for the Democrats, had a powerful effect on the electorate. Indeed, Johnson won by a landslide.

Now that he had been elected president by the people he believed he could get his proposals through Congress. He immediately initiated his "Great Society" program, which was supposed to help the lower- and middle-class American and end poverty in the United States. In fact, it included several social-welfare programs that resembled certain programs that had been initiated by President Franklin Delano Roosevelt, whom he admired.

The Wilderness Areas Act, which set aside millions of acres of land primarily for the public, was passed. In short, economic development of these acres was prohibited. The Mass Transit Act, which provided funding for subways, buses, and commuter train systems, was passed. The National Defense Education Act, which provided funding for educational purposes, was passed..

In 1965 the Elementary and Secondary Education Act was passed. This act provided funding to improve education at each level. The same year President Johnson pressed leading members of Congress to expand Social Security by including what became known as Medicare and Medicaid.[1] The former provided health insurance to seniors for a nominal cost. The latter covered healthcare for those who were considered poor. The Appalachian Regional Development Act, which encouraged economic development in the mountainous areas in the southeastern United States, was passed the same year. The Head Start Act, which provided educational opportunity for the poor, was passed the same year. The Voting Rights Act, which provided every legal-aged American the right to vote, was passed the same year. This act was in reaction to the states that had established codes or laws that prevented African-Americans from voting.

In 1966 the Demonstration Cities and Metropolitan Development Act was passed and provided funds for abolishing depressed areas in cities, improving landscaping, creating parks, and improving urban areas.

The Clean Water Restoration Act was passed the same year and allocated billions of dollars for control projects.

In 1967 the Higher Education Act was passed and provided educational opportunity for the poor or less affluent. The Omnibus Housing Act was passed in 1968. This act provided funding for housing to be built for poor and middle-income families. Later the same year the Housing and Urban Development Act, which expanded the Omnibus Housing Act, was passed. Additional legislation included another Civil Rights bill that strengthened the previous Civil Rights bill by attempting to eliminate discrimination in the rental or sale of apartments, condominiums, and houses because of religion, national origin, or race.

As if the above were not enough, the Department of Housing and Urban Development and the Department of Transportation were established. In addition, the National Endowment for the Humanities and the Arts was funded. The Corporation for Public Broadcasting was funded as well.

Although several of his domestic programs were accepted by the public, his foreign policies, which contradicted Kennedy's in the sense that his policies welcomed military dictatorships in Latin America and escalated the war in Vietnam, were not. For instance, when people rebelled in the Dominican Republic, he ordered military troops to suppress the rebellion.

In 1964 the United States contributed additional aid and more military advisers to South Vietnam. When North Vietnamese PT Boats reportedly fired on an American destroyer in the Gulf of Tonkin, Johnson immediately ordered retaliatory air strikes against North Vietnamese torpedo-boat bases. This, together with Congressional approval to assist the South Vietnamese to prevent Viet Cong aggression, encouraged Johnson not only to bomb North Vietnam but to send almost 200,000 American soldiers before 1966. As Johnson's determination to end what he believed was Chinese expansion hardened, more than 500,000 American soldiers were fighting what inevitably became a seemingly endless war by 1968.

His so-called "Great Society" had become one of confusion. Indeed, disillusionment set in, especially among the young. Protests, particularly on college and university campuses, appeared across the country. The citizenry grew divided over various issues while funding of the war increased, causing spiraling inflation. Johnson was severely criticized by the public and eventually the press. In fact, the Vietnam War resembled a cancer growing in the United States. As more military units were sent, as more military personnel were killed or wounded, as more military equipment was destroyed, and as more money was spent, more and more young people demonstrated against the war.

The Vietnam War, which did not end until Johnson was out of office, affected millions of Americans who served in the military primarily because the war lasted years—from about 1954 to 1975. The war, itself, was expensive, costing more than $100 billion. This does not include the enormous amount of taxpayer money that was spent on accepting hundreds of thousands of Vietnamese, Laotians, and Cambodians who immigrated to the United States after the war ended.

To say the least, President Johnson enjoyed spending taxpayer money and increasing the national debt. Although his Great Society program was expensive, his escalating the war in Vietnam only added to the nation's expenditures during his years in office.

In 1968, when Johnson realized that the majority of Americans, including elected as well as appointed officials, opposed his policies in Vietnam, he announced that he would not seek reelection.

Unfortunately, the war in Vietnam raged on. Eugene McCarthy and Robert Kennedy sought the presidential nomination within the Democratic Party. However, Robert Kennedy was murdered in California. Hubert Humphrey, perhaps the wrong politician for the Democrats primarily because his views were not that dissimilar to Johnson's, received the nomination. The Republicans nominated Richard M. Nixon who had conducted an impressive campaign. Governor George Wallace of Alabama was a third presidential candidate, running on the American Independent Party ticket. Although the votes cast for the Democratic and Republican candidates were closely divided (Nixon received only 500,000 more popular votes than Humphrey), he received more than 100 electoral votes than Humphrey.

Richard Nixon had been born in California and had worked in his father's store. He had graduated from Whittier College and the Duke University Law School. During World War II he had worked as an attorney for the federal government and then had served as an officer in the United States Navy.

In 1946 he had been elected to the House of Representatives. Four years later he had been elected to the United States Senate. In 1952 he had been nominated for vice president by the Republicans. Dwight David Eisenhower had been nominated for president. When Eisenhower had been elected president, Nixon had served as his vice president and had traveled extensively on his behalf.

In 1960 he had been nominated for president by the Republicans, but he had lost by a narrow margin to President John F. Kennedy. Two years later he had run for governor of California, but he had lost to Edward "Pat" Brown, a Democrat.

Nixon had moved to New York City and had practiced law. However, within four years he had reemerged as the leader of the Republican Party and had been nominated for president in 1968. His campaign had focused on a balanced budget, an end to the war in Vietnam, and law and order.

As president, Richard Nixon faced division at home over the Vietnam War, civil rights, and an unstable economy. Almost immediately he set into motion a policy called Vietnamization. The policy reduced the number of Americans serving in Vietnam from more than 500,000 in 1968 to some 60,000 by the last quarter of 1972. Still, the policy was criticized by certain Democrats in Congress as well as specific groups in the United States because it allowed more American soldiers to be killed. Nixon also ordered the bombing of Cambodia, which Hanoi had been using to send supplies as well as troops to the borders of South Vietnam. This action stirred the emotions of college and university students who demonstrated on college and university campuses. As a result, several students who were involved in the demonstrations were killed by National Guardsmen and police officers and more than 20 were wounded. Members of Congress received calls from angry constituents.

Nixon slashed the spending on the war. The Gulf of Tonkin resolution was repealed. When the so-called Pentagon Papers, which concerned the war in Vietnam primarily during the previous presidential administration, appeared in the *New York Times* in 1971, readers realized that their government had lied to them about the war. When such atrocities as the My Lai incident were revealed by the press, Americans questioned the military's actions in the war.

Unperturbed, Nixon increased and widened the bombing. The efforts failed, however. Peace negotiations, which had been discussed for months, failed because of disagreements over Thieu's role in South Vietnam. Nixon ordered bombs to be dropped on Hanoi and Haiphong. Eventually, this action persuaded Hanoi and Thieu to reach a cease-fire settlement. The agreement, called the Paris Accords, was immediately broken when Thieu failed to allow the Viet Cong to participate in South Vietnam policies. Consequently, Hanoi bombed South Vietnam from 1973 to 1975, until Thieu and Lon Nol conceded South Vietnam and Cambodia, respectively, to North Vietnam.

Although Nixon's primary goal in Vietnam had been to achieve peace with honor, peace eventually occurred, but it was not necessarily with honor. Of course, Nixon had inherited what had been a civil war in a country where political policies and a philosophy of life differed greatly from those of the United States. These differences should have been reason enough for the United States not getting involved in the war whatsoever.

It is possible that more American soldiers' lives may have been saved had the Nixon administration not changed its negotiating positions which had called for the withdrawal of North Vietnamese troops from South Vietnam.

There had been countless demonstrations on college and university campuses primarily because of the war in Vietnam. Nixon had promised to bring American soldiers home, which he did. However, it had taken more than one term.

In 1972 he campaigned against George McGovern and George Wallace. While campaigning, Wallace was wounded in an assassination attempt. Disabled, Wallace could not proceed with his campaign.

McGovern's vice presidential candidate, Senator Thomas Eagleton, resigned from the Democratic ticket because of the media's coverage of his psychiatric treatment. Unfortunately, the press coverage of Eagleton apparently tarnished McGovern. Nixon easily defeated him, but the Republicans did not hold the House of Representatives or the Senate of the United States after the election.

Nixon reversed the nation's policy toward Red China when he accepted an invitation to visit that country in 1972. Encouraging positive relations with the Chinese People's Republic, he had discussions regarding Taiwan with Chinese leaders Mao Tse-tung and Chou En-lai. Later the same year he flew to Moscow where he discussed limiting strategic weapons with Leonid Brezhnev, the leader of the Soviet Union. Although the Strategic Arms Limitations Talks (SALT I) did not limit the manufacturing of nuclear weapons, an agreement between the two powers was reached on what could be built.

The relationship between Israel and the United States and the relationship between Syria and the Soviet Union caused détente to splinter when Egypt and Syria, supported with Soviet weapons, attacked Israel in 1973. The United States, which had made commitments to Israel, supported her with weapons. Unfortunately, the Organization of Petroleum Exporting Countries (OPEC), which was controlled by the Arab nations, placed a ban on oil to western Europe and the United States two weeks after the war started. Such action forced the United States and the Middle Eastern nations to a settlement. Secretary of State Henry Kissinger, with his so-called "shuttle diplomacy," aided in negotiations which forced a cease-fire between Israel and Egypt and between Israel and Syria in 1974.

Concurrently, President Nixon's domestic policies failed to achieve prosperity for the United States. Of course, the Vietnam War caused many of the domestic problems, particularly inflation. His first so-called "game plan" included controlling money and unusually high interest rates, which together produced a recession. However, inflation, because of expenditures related to the war as well as less money from fewer exports, increased the cost of living. As the volume of exports declined, industrial production decreased. Subsequently, unemployment increased. Nixon instituted wage and price controls and devalued the dollar. Although the trade deficit improved, inflation continued but at a slower rate of increase, which slightly improved the economy.

When five men were apprehended after breaking into the Democratic National Committee headquarters at the Watergate building in Washington, D.C., a chain of events, which included connections between the burglars and certain members of the White House staff, ultimately led to Nixon's resignation in 1974.

The burglars had been hired by the Committee for the Reelection of the President (CREEP). Although they were apprehended during the act, which occurred in 1972 before the presidential election, the event had no effect on Nixon's integrity or reelection primarily because the trial had not started. Still, reporters from the press wrote stories about the burglary and its aftermath. In addition, District Court Judge John J. Sirica, who presided over the eventual case of the burglars, encouraged them to provide information about everyone involved before they were sentenced. As a result, he learned there were ties to the White House from one of the accused.

The United States Senate established the Select Committee on Presidential Campaign Activities, which was chaired by Senator Sam Ervin, to primarily learn about any corruption that may have occurred during the previous election. What members of the committee eventually learned was worse than what they had expected. The burglars, who were called "plumbers," had been organized by several members of the White House staff primarily to conduct illegal activities. The committee also learned about the White House's plan to cover up the break-in at the Watergate building. As if this was not bad enough, one or more individuals who worked with the president informed members of the committee about other misdeeds. The committee submitted their report, which contained damaging information about the White House and the president.

Other incidents damaged the presidency as well, including indictments against former Attorney General John Mitchell, who had provided approval of G. Gordon Liddy's basic spy operation, and White House staff members, John Ehrlichman, Charles Colson, H. R.

Haldeman, and a few others. In addition, the press attacked Nixon's vice president, Spiro Agnew, who had been accused of accepting bribes from contractors when he had been the governor of Maryland. As a result of the case against him, Agnew resigned from the vice presidency in 1973.

After seriously considering one or more individuals for the vice president's position, Nixon chose Congressman Gerald Ford of Michigan. Ford accepted and was confirmed by Congress in late 1973.

Although Nixon had recorded conversations in the Oval Office of the White House, which he intended to keep private, a few were released to the press. When District Court Judge Sirica learned about these recordings, he provided the subpoenas for the tapes. The House Judiciary Committee, which had been holding hearings on impeachment, charged President Nixon on three articles. Nixon realized that his second term had come to an abrupt end. Instead of fighting the Democrats, he resigned on August 9, 1974. Vice President Gerald Ford became president.

Gerald R. Ford had been born Leslie King, Jr. in Nebraska, but had grown up in Michigan primarily because his mother had divorced his father and had married another man. Gerald had been adopted by his stepfather and had taken his name.

Ford had graduated from the University of Michigan and from the Law School at Yale University. He had practiced law and had served as an officer in the United States Navy during World War II.

He had been elected to the United States House of Representatives in 1948. He had been a member of the Warren Commission and had been named minority leader of the House in 1965.

In 1973, after Vice President Agnew had resigned, President Nixon had nominated him for vice president. Ford had been confirmed by both houses of Congress.

Although he had spoken openly in support of President Nixon, the House of Representatives had developed three articles of impeachment against him. Eventually, primarily because Nixon had lacked support of the Congress and the public, he had resigned in 1974.

Gerald R. Ford was respected by Republicans and Democrats alike. However, he was the first man to serve as president who was not elected by the people. As president, he immediately pardoned President Nixon for any violations of federal law he may have committed while serving as president. The public was shocked. Ford was severely criticized by leading members of Congress. Although this criticism was personal and certainly affected him, he did not have time to worry about it primarily because the economy was getting weaker. Indeed, inflation was rising and unemployment was increasing seemingly every day.

Ford responded by introducing an anti-inflation program called "Whip Inflation Now" (WIN), but his proposals basically failed. Indeed, during 1974 and 1975, the nation faced its worst recession since the 1930s. The trade deficit increased, industrial production decreased, and unemployment increased to more than eight percent. Before he left office, however, the rate of inflation had actually decreased.

It must be mentioned that Ford was not necessarily responsible for these problems. For instance, he signed bills that actually lowered taxes in an effort to stimulate the economy. He also signed bills that lowered interest rates. On the other hand, he vetoed bills that would have increased employment and extended welfare programs, among others. These bills may have helped the economy in the short term, but not necessarily in the long term. Welfare programs, for instance, only add to the national debt. In the long term, such programs generally cause problems for a nation's economy.

Because of OPEC's quadrupling of oil prices, the Ford administration was forced to make decisions regarding issues previous presidents and their administrations had never faced. Controversy over off-shore oil explorations, the Alaskan pipeline, and strip mining for coal aroused not only the public but Congress. Environmental protection became a major topic that was discussed. The Ford administration favored deregulation of prices on energy sources because high prices undoubtedly would lower consumption. Of course, this position was the opposite of the position of certain Democrats. They believed that deregulation would increase corporate profits at the consumer's expense. Perhaps as a compromise the Energy Policy and Conservation Act, which concerned energy conservation as well as alternative energy sources, was passed by Congress in 1975.

Ford's foreign policy was similar to Nixon's. Henry Kissinger was retained as secretary of state and continued the Strategic Arms Limitation Talks (SALT). Unfortunately, these talks produced few agreements.

A five-year trade agreement concerning grain was signed by the major powers in 1975, and Kissinger was responsible for a $10 billion arms sale to Iran in 1976.

In 1975 Hanoi ordered a major offensive against South Vietnam and Cambodia. As a result, Ford attempted to persuade Congress to provide almost one billion dollars in aid to both countries, but Congress refused. The American public had had enough of Vietnam. Ford declared the Vietnam War was over. In reality, primarily because Congress had tied the president's hands with the War Powers Resolution, which required presidents to inform Congress about any military troops being sent or reinforced overseas, Ford had to watch as people, including officials of the United States and South Vietnam, scrambled to helicopters from the rooftop of the United States Embassy in Saigon. South Vietnam fell to the Communists. The same happened in Cambodia and Laos. Hundreds of thousands of people had been killed.

In addition to the War Powers Resolution, Congress passed additional acts that limited the president's deployment of the military or exporting arms to other countries.

Ford attempted to produce something positive before the presidential election. He discussed arms with Leonid Brezhnev, the leader of the Soviet Union, which resulted in an agreement to reduce the number of offensive intercontinental ballistic missiles and defensive antiballistic missiles.

Ford's wife, Betty, unlike previous First Ladies, was very candid with reporters. In fact, she even informed them about her health, including her problems with alcohol. Many people who learned about her issues appreciated her openness.

Primarily because he had pardoned President Nixon, Ford was defeated by Jimmy Carter. Carter, a Democrat, was the former governor of Georgia.

Jimmy Carter had grown up on a farm in Plains, Georgia, and had attended Southwestern College, the Georgia Institute of Technology, and the United States Naval Academy, from which he had graduated in 1946. He had married Rosalynn Smith and later had focused on a career in the United States Navy, but his father's death had caused him to resign his commission and return to Georgia to manage the farm.

In 1962 he had been elected to the state senate of Georgia. In 1966 he had campaigned for the governorship of the state, but had lost. Depressed, he had become a born-again Christian. In 1970 he had run a second time for the governorship and had won. In 1974, before his term as governor had ended, he had announced his candidacy for president. He had labeled himself as an outsider and had campaigned well.

In 1976 he had won the Democratic nomination and had chosen Senator Walter Mondale of Minnesota as his running mate. The presidential election had been close.

As president, Carter was more informal than previous presidents. Still, he attempted to restore integrity to the office. Human rights underlined his domestic and foreign policies, and he even established a Bureau of Human Rights in the State Department.

A day after his inauguration he pardoned draft evaders who had escaped the horrors of the Vietnam War by leaving the country or by not informing the federal government of their whereabouts. Certain groups severely criticized him for this action, but he believed the pardon was the first step in healing the nation from the scars inflicted on it by the war.

He introduced numerous programs that would have reformed society and the economy, but the Democratic Congress opposed most of them. Certain members of Congress realized they had more power than the president. After all, they had exhibited it by ridding themselves of President Nixon. Besides, who did Jimmy Carter think he was, anyway? He had never served as a member of Congress or the Senate. Nor had he served as a member of a presidential cabinet. Still, he persuaded Congress to enact legislation that would fund a Department of Energy. He also asked for conservative measures to be implemented, including an excise tax on automobiles with poor gas mileage, increased taxes on domestic oil, a tax on gasoline, tax incentives to encourage businesses to use another form of energy, and tax incentives to encourage homeowners to use insulation.

However, the country's economy worsened. As a result, his popularity among the people declined quickly. In addition, in 1977 the director of the Office of Management and Budget, Bert Lance, was accused of financial mismanagement when he had worked in Georgia. Carter initially supported his friend. Eventually, primarily because of the continued negative coverage by the press, he asked Lance to resign, which he did.

Although the press ran numerous stories about Lance, Carter's younger brother, Billy, was soon the subject of headlines. Billy, who enjoyed drinking beer, lived and worked in Georgia. He allowed several reporters to interview him primarily because he was not like his older brother, Jimmy. Later, in 1980, Billy's purported connection to the government of Libya would be an embarrassment to the president.

Carter was more successful in foreign affairs than he was in domestic ones—at least, for a while. For instance, in 1977 his administration was responsible for two treaties between the United States and Panama. The first basically gave Panama control of the Panama Canal at the end of 1999. The second basically guaranteed that the canal would be neutral after 1999. However, his attempt to force the Soviet Union to change its human rights policies failed.

In 1978 the Shah of Iran, who had been in power since 1954, was overthrown by an Islamic revolution headed by Ayatollah Khomeini. This was an embarrassment to the United States primarily because the federal government had supported the Shah for decades. On the other hand, President Anwar el-Sadat of Egypt and Prime Minister Menachem Begin of Israel had discussed peace, but disagreements between the two had ended the talks in 1978. The same year Carter invited both leaders to Camp David to discuss peace between the two countries. After several days of discussions, an agreement, which was called the Camp David Accords, was reached, thus ending the hostility between the two nations.

In 1979 Carter established diplomatic relations between the United States and China. Although he was criticized for developing anti-Soviet ties with the Communist country, he and Leonid Brezhnev, the leader of the Soviet Union, signed a new Strategic Arms Limitation Treaty (SALT II). However, when the Soviet Union invaded Afghanistan several months later, Carter removed the treaty from consideration by the United States Senate. In addition, he insisted that the United States boycott the 1980 Summer Olympics primarily because the games were being held in Moscow, Russia. Although Carter was criticized by spokespersons for various groups, he remained firm in his insistence.

Unfortunately, also in 1979, the Shah of Iran fled his country. Although warned, Carter allowed him to enter the United States. The same year Iranian students, with the support of Ayatollah Khomeini, broke into the United States Embassy in Teheran and took the diplomats and staff members hostage. Although Carter tried to negotiate the release of the hostages, he was not successful. Later, he approved a military operation that was supposed to rescue the hostages, but the operation failed. Needless to say, he and his administration were humiliated.

As if this was not grave enough, OPEC increased the price of oil going to foreign countries. Carter encouraged Congress to pass legislation that would fund alternative fuels, including wind and solar, which it did.

Unfortunately, the little legislation that he had encouraged Congress to pass to help the economy had failed. In fact, the inflation rate, which had decreased to less than five percent when Carter became president, quadrupled before he left office four years later. Interest rates soared because of Carter's unwillingness to implement controls on wages, prices, and interest rates. Unemployment increased because of decreased industrial production. The value of the dollar declined, while trade deficits increased dramatically. Of course, Carter's terrible economy was caused in part by the energy crisis, which actually had started earlier in the 1970s. At the time, the United States was dependent on foreign oil.[2]

In late 1979, after a meeting at Camp David, Carter informed the American people they needed to lower their expectations and conserve energy. Senator Edward Kennedy of Massachusetts realized that Carter was vulnerable and decided to seek the Democratic nomination for president in 1980, but Carter prevailed at the Democratic National Convention.

However, Ronald W. Reagan, a former actor and governor of California who had been a Democrat years before and who had become a Republican, was that party's candidate for president. Reagan easily defeated Carter and John Anderson, a Republican who ran as an Independent, in November. Apparently, the American people had had enough of Jimmy Carter. Reagan had won the presidency in a landslide. In fact, he had been popular among men and women, no matter their age, income, or where they lived. Only the majority of African-Americans and Jews had voted for Carter.

Before he left office, President Carter signed legislation that set aside millions of acres of land in Alaska so it could not be developed.

Jimmy and Rosalynn returned to Georgia, where they established the Carter Presidential Center in Atlanta. In addition, he served the nation as an unofficial peace maker. He also helped build numerous homes through the Habitat for Humanity, a charitable organization. He also wrote numerous books.

Ronald Reagan had been born in Illinois and had lived with his parents in several towns, including Dixon, Illinois, where he had attended school. Reagan had played football, studied economics and sociology, and had been active in dramatics at Eureka College, in Eureka, Illinois, from which he had graduated in 1932. Reagan had worked as a sportscaster in Iowa before he had traveled to California to take a screen test at Warner Brothers. Reagan had become an actor and had appeared in numerous films over the years. He had married Jane Wyman, an actress, and had a daughter and had adopted a son. He and Jane had divorced in 1948.

During World War II Reagan had served as an officer and had made training films for the military. After the war he had resumed his acting career and had served as president of the Screen Actors Guild. He had testified before the House Un-American Activities Committee, which had investigated individuals who had been accused of being Communists or Communist sympathizers. Reagan had been criticized for his cooperation with the committee.

In 1949 Reagan had met Nancy Davis, a struggling actress. They had married four years later and eventually had two children.

For decades Reagan had been a Democrat. However, primarily because he had grown more conservative, he had supported Dwight David Eisenhower for president in the 1950s and had spoken on behalf of Richard Nixon in 1960.

Reagan had hosted the *General Electric Theater*, a drama series on television, and had spoken to employees of the company throughout the country.

In 1964 he had spoken in support of Barry Goldwater, the Republican candidate for president. The speech had brought him national attention. Two years later he had run for the governorship of California and had won. He had served two terms. Although he had challenged Gerald Ford for the nomination of president in 1976, he had not been successful.

Four years later, however, he had become the Republican nominee and had chosen George H. W. Bush as his running mate. He had easily defeated Jimmy Carter and John Anderson.

Reagan, unlike many presidents, knew how to tell a joke and often did. He also knew how to put complicated economic information into everyday language, so every American adult could understand it. This is one reason he was called the "Great Communicator."

When Reagan became president, Iran immediately released the American hostages. Soon after, John W. Hinckley, Jr., fired several shots at Reagan, hitting him in the chest and hitting a few others, including Press Secretary James Brady. Reagan and Brady were severely wounded and were rushed to the hospital. Reagan slowly recovered, but Brady was disabled.

When he was released, Reagan proposed tax cuts and reductions in welfare and unemployment programs. Concurrently, he proposed an increase in defense spending. He cut several federal agencies that, in his view, limited business growth. Congress approved most of his proposals, including the Economic Recovery Tax Act of 1981, which lowered individual and corporation income taxes. Additional cuts in taxes were scheduled for the future. This was the largest cut in income taxes in the nation's history.

Later the same year thousands of members of the Professional Air Traffic Controllers Organization (PATCO) went on strike, which was against the law for federal employees. Although they wanted more money and better working conditions, President Reagan told them to return to work. When most of the members refused, he fired them.

In 1982 the nation experienced a recession. Several thousand businesses were forced to file for bankruptcy. Unemployment rose to more than 10 percent of the work force. The trade deficit increased. The federal budget deficit increased, too, primarily because there had not been enough cuts in spending. Of course, there was another reason—social security. Indeed, social security benefits, which had been raised by Congress numerous times over the years, accounted for more than 20 percent of the total federal budget when Reagan became president. He was not necessarily interested in decreasing benefits to people, especially seniors. Consequently, social security benefits continued to make up a large percentage of the federal budget.

President Reagan and Congress reacted by increasing taxes. By the middle of 1983 the recession was under control and the nation was recovering. In fact, inflation and unemployment had been reduced. Reagan's economic policies continued to work for the nation throughout his years in the White House. However, his policies were criticized for helping the wealthy and harming the poor. African-Americans, women, and conservationists criticized him the most, even though he was the first president to appoint a woman, Sandra Day O'Connor, to the United States Supreme Court. In addition, he was the first president to appoint three women to Cabinet-level positions at the same time. His secretary of the interior, James G. Watt, encouraged the weakening of certain environmental regulations concerning air, water, and wildlife, however. Because of severe criticism, Watt resigned in 1983.

The same year the Reagan administration became involved in the withdrawal of Palestine Liberation Organization (PLO) units from Lebanon. Then several United States Marine Corps units joined a peacekeeping force in Lebanon. Unfortunately, a year later terrorists bombed the headquarters of the United States Marine Corps, which was located at the airport of Beirut, killing more than 240 servicemen. In 1984, primarily because certain Lebanese groups increased fighting in Beirut, the Reagan administration moved the troops of the United States from Beirut to offshore ships.

Rebellions in Nicaragua and El Salvador became a major problem in the early 1980s as well. Reagan sent economic and military assistance, including advisers and arms, to the rebels in Nicaragua and to the government in El Salvador. Grenada was invaded by American troops in 1983, after Grenadian rebels overthrew the island's government. Reagan told the American public that the invasion had been necessary to protect American lives and to halt Cuba's intention to use the island as a military base.

Reagan was strongly opposed to Communism. This is the primary reason he supported the military so strongly. In 1983 the Soviet Union shot down a Korean airliner that had departed Alaska for Korea. As a result, 269 people were killed. The Soviet Union claimed the airliner had flown into its territory. Reagan, who had proposed the Strategic Defense Initiative (SDI), which was a space-based missile defense system, in 1982, made certain the proposal was discussed in the press, so Mikhail Gorbachev, the leader of the Soviet Union, would learn about it. In fact, Gorbachev believed Reagan's proposal would cause an escalation of the Cold War. In reality, Gorbachev realized the Soviet Union was not in an economic position to support such a counter military initiative in space. Consequently, by proposing this military system, Reagan helped the United States win the Cold War. Without question, more than any other president, he helped cause the Soviet Union to collapse.

In 1984 Walter F. Mondale and Geraldine A. Ferraro were nominated by the Democrats, but they were easily defeated by Reagan and George Bush. A cancerous tumor was found in Reagan's colon, and many Americans grew concerned about his health. He recovered, however, primarily because of his physical condition.

In 1985 the National Security Council (NSC), located in the White House, sold military weapons to Iran in exchange for the country's help in getting American hostages out of Lebanon. Of course, this action was against the nation's policy regarding terrorism. Then millions of dollars earned from the sale of arms were used to purchase military weapons for the Contras in Nicaragua. When the press learned about the Iran-Contra Affair, President Reagan was embarrassed, to say the least. He fired Lieutenant Colonel Oliver North of the United States Marines and Rear Admiral John Poindexter, who was head of the NSC. Apparently, both had been involved.

Reagan appointed a special commission that was chaired by former Senator John Tower of Texas to investigate the affair. The House of Representatives and the Senate of the United States held hearings about the sale of arms to Iran and the military assistance to the Contras in Nicaragua. As a result of the hearings being covered by the press, the American people learned about the affair.

Although Reagan accepted responsibility for the sale of arms to Iran, he denied knowing anything about the military assistance to the Contras.

Also in 1985 Reagan met with Gorbachev in Switzerland to discuss nuclear missiles. They met again a year later in Iceland to discuss reducing nuclear missiles. However, they could not reach an agreement. In 1987 they met again and signed the INF Treaty which eliminated intermediate-range nuclear missiles in Europe.

Although sound, the economy slowed during 1985. Congress passed the Tax Reform Act, which basically simplified income taxes on individuals and corporations, in 1986. This action, together with a healthy economy, helped reduce the federal budget deficit for 1987. However, when the stock market crashed in October 1987, Reagan and Congress agreed to raise taxes.

Acts of terror increased in the latter 1980s. When terrorists bombed a nightclub in West Berlin in 1986, Reagan placed economic sanctions on Libya and froze the country's assets in the United States. He charged General Muammar al-Qaddafi and the Libyan government with sponsoring acts of terrorism. When Libya fired missiles at American military planes, the United States military responded, attacking Libyan missile installations and ships. Later, the United States military conducted air strikes against military targets in the Libyan cities of Tripoli and Benghazi.

In 1987 United States warships were fired upon by Iran's military. Reagan immediately ordered a military response and subsequently ended trade between the United States and Iran. Then an Iraqi military plane fired two missiles at a warship in the Persian Gulf, killing almost 40 crew members. In 1988 an Iranian civilian airliner, which had been mistaken for a warplane, was shot down by an American warship. Almost 300 people were killed.

In 1988 Reagan supported George H. W. Bush, the Republican nominee for president, who easily defeated the Democratic candidate, Michael Dukakis. When Reagan left the White House, he and Nancy returned to California. His autobiography, *An American Life*, was published in 1990.

Four years later he informed the American people that he had Alzheimer disease.

George H. W. Bush had grown up in Connecticut and had graduated from Phillips Academy in Andover, Massachusetts. He had served as a bomber pilot in the Pacific during World War II and had been shot down in 1944.

A year later he had married Barbara Pierce.

He had graduated from Yale University and, later, had moved his family to Texas, where he had co-founded several companies. Later, he had run for the United States Senate in 1964 and again in 1970. He had been defeated both times by the Democratic candidate. However, he had been elected in 1966 to the House of Representatives of the United States.

Bush had served as the United States ambassador to the United Nations, as chairman of the Republican National Committee, and as the head of the United States Liaison Office in China in the early 1970s. In 1976 he had served as the director of the Central Intelligence Agency (CIA).

Although Bush had announced his candidacy for president in 1979, he had ended his campaign when Ronald Reagan became a popular candidate among Republicans. Bush had supported Reagan and Reagan had chosen Bush as his running mate.

As vice president, Bush had traveled extensively all over the world.

As president, Bush intended to continue Reagan's domestic economic program, but he faced a nightmare in the early days of his presidency. In addition to the negative publicity of the Iran-Contra Affair, more than a thousand savings and loan institutions failed during the 1980s, while hundreds more faced bankruptcy.

There was little that Bush could do about the negative publicity concerning the Iran-Contra Affair. Indeed, the press covered each person's trial. For instance, in 1989 a federal grand jury convicted Lieutenant Colonel Oliver North of interfering with Congress's investigation of the Iran-Contra Affair. An appeals court overturned North's conviction on the mishandling of documents charge. The court also ordered a lower court to reexamine the evidence used to convict North on the other charges. The case against North was ultimately dismissed in 1991.

John Poindexter was convicted of conspiracy and lying to and obstructing Congress in its investigation of the affair in 1990. An appeals court overturned his conviction in 1991. Casper Weinberger, who had served as President Reagan's secretary of defense, was charged in 1992 with lying to Congress and to federal investigators who were investigating the Iran-Contra Affair. President Bush pardoned Weinberger and others for any crimes they may have committed in relation to the Iran-Contra Affair.

However, for the savings and loan industry, Bush proposed legislation that would hopefully rescue the remaining savings and loans. The Financial Institutions Reform, Recovery, and Enforcement Act, which cost taxpayers billions of dollars, was enacted in 1989.

Unfortunately, as if the savings and loan industry was not bad enough, the tanker *Exxon Valdez* spilled more than 10 million gallons of crude oil near Valdez, Alaska, in 1989. Fishermen and the public became outraged as a result of the pollution. Bush ordered the military to take charge of the cleanup operation.

The same year grand juries in Florida indicted General Manuel Noriega, the brutal leader of Panama who was involved in a drug-smuggling operation. Authorities demanded that Noriega be extradited to the United States to stand trial, but Noriega refused. Immediately, Bush imposed economic sanctions against Panama. Then he ordered the United States military to invade Panama to capture Noriega. Noriega was arrested in 1990 and taken to Miami, Florida. He was convicted of drug smuggling in 1992 and sentenced to prison.

In 1990 President Bush met with Mikhail Gorbachev, the leader of the Soviet Union, in Washington, D.C., and the two signed an agreement to reduce nuclear weapons. The same year an economic recession occurred in the United States, and Bush, working with Congress, raised taxes, which he had promised not to do when he had campaigned for president two years before. However, unemployment increased. By the middle of 1991 seven percent of the nation's workforce was unemployed. Bush urged bank regulators to lower interest rates. The economy improved with time, but unemployment remained high.

Also in 1990 Bush signed a bill that amended the Clean Air Act of 1970. The amendment set stricter standards for air quality and emissions.

Unfortunately, in addition to the weak economy, other problems such as drug abuse, homelessness, and violent crime, plagued American cities. Certain critics blamed the president for allowing such problems to exist even though Bush had to deal with a Democratic Congress.

In August 1990, Saddam Hussein, the dictator of Iraq, ordered his military to invade Kuwait, an oil-rich country. Bush, with Margaret Thatcher's support, organized an international coalition of armed forces. In November 1990, the Security Council of the United Nations authorized coalition members to use whatever means necessary to expel Iraq from Kuwait. Hussein was given until the middle of January 1991, to withdraw his troops. He refused, however, and Bush initiated Operation Desert Storm. Iraqi military targets were bombed. Then the huge coalition army attacked Hussein's army, defeating it within days. As a result, General Norman Schwarzkopf, the American commander, and General Colin Powell, the chairman of the Joint Chiefs of Staff, became household names. When Kuwait's independence was restored, Bush was satisfied. Primarily because he did not order troops to capture Hussein, Bush was severely criticized. In April, Bush ordered American troops into northern Iraq to work with other coalition forces in establishing a safety zone for Kurdish refugees. The Kurds had rebelled soon after Iraq's defeat in the Gulf War. The rebellion had been squashed by Iraqi troops, however, and the Kurds had fled to the mountains. The United States provided the Kurds with food and other necessities until July. Most of the Kurds had returned to their homes or to other countries by that time.

Bush met with Mikhail Gorbachev, the leader of the Soviet Union, in 1990 and 1991. They agreed to destroy most of their chemical weapons. They signed a nonaggression pact and the Strategic Arms Reduction Treaty (START I), which reduced the number of long-range nuclear bombers and missiles. They also pressured leaders of the Middle East to discuss peace.

In 1991 Bush announced the United States would reduce its short-range nuclear weapons. The Soviet Union did the same. The same year Bush announced the United States would establish full diplomatic relations with the Baltic States. Before 1992, the nations that had made up the Soviet Union declared their independence. Thus, the Soviet Union ceased to exist. Many of the nations formed the Commonwealth of Independent States.

President Bush met with Russian President Boris Yeltsin and they signed the START II Treaty, which cut each country's number of long-range nuclear weapons to less than half the number proposed in START I.

In 1992 Bush and other world leaders agreed to provide Russia with economic aid. The same year rioting erupted in Los Angeles after a jury decided not to convict four white Los Angeles police officers who had assaulted African-American Rodney King. King had been pursued by the police for blocks. The rioting occurred primarily in African-American neighborhoods and resulted in more than 50 deaths and more than one billion dollars in property damage. Bush sent several thousand troops and law enforcement officers to Los Angeles to help restore order.

A federal jury convicted two of the police officers for violating King's civil rights in 1993.

Later in 1992 the North American Free Trade Agreement (NAFTA) was signed. Eventually, this eliminated tariffs and other trade barriers between the United States, Canada, and Mexico.

In late 1992 the nation's economy had not recovered. Billionaire H. Ross Perot of Texas mentioned this fact, among others, on television. As a result of his candor, Perot became popular among the public. In addition to William (Bill) Jefferson Clinton becoming the Democratic candidate for president, Perot ran as a third-party candidate. As if these candidates were not enough of a challenge, Bush had to defeat Patrick Buchanan, another Republican, for the party's nomination. Although Bush eventually got the nod from the Republicans, he was defeated by Clinton. Without question, the reason Bush lost the presidency was because of Perot, especially if one looks at the percentages of votes each candidate received: Clinton received 43 percent of the votes; Bush received 37 percent of the votes; and Perot received 19 percent of the votes.

Bill Clinton's father had been killed in an automobile accident before Bill had been born. His mother had married Roger Clinton and, later, Clinton had taken his stepfather's name.

Clinton had become interested in politics by the time he had met President John F. Kennedy in 1963. A year later he had enrolled at Georgetown University in Washington, D.C. As an undergraduate he had been elected president of the student body and had worked as an intern for Senator J. William Fulbright of Arkansas. Clinton had graduated in 1968 and had attended the University of Oxford as a Rhodes Scholar. Later, he had attended the law school at Yale University, from which he had graduated in 1973.

Clinton had taught law at the University of Arkansas School of Law and had run an unsuccessful campaign for the House of Representatives of the United States in 1974. A year later he had married Hillary Rodham. In 1976 Clinton had been elected attorney general of Arkansas. Two years later he had been elected governor of the state.

Although he had lost the governorship in 1980, he had been elected to the office in 1982. In fact, he had been governor when he had announced his candidacy for president.

Unfortunately, Clinton entered the White House amid allegations that he had had an extramarital affair while he served as governor of Arkansas. Unshaken, he immediately appointed his wife to oversee the Task Force on National Healthcare Reform. He was criticized for nepotism. She was criticized for her seemingly radical views about women's health issues. However, the eventual Health Security Act was not passed by Congress primarily because of its cost to employers and taxpayers, not necessarily because of the criticism of the president or his wife.

Clinton signed the Family Medical Leave Act, which required employers to provide employees with up to three months of unpaid leave for family and medical emergencies.

Clinton appointed women and minorities to specific positions in his administration. For instance, after his first two choices for attorney general withdrew because of financial improprieties relating to their childcare workers, Janet Reno was confirmed. In addition, Donna Shalala became the secretary of Health and Human Services and Joycelyn Elders became the surgeon general. Later, several of his cabinet members, including Deputy Secretary of the Treasury Roger Altman and Secretary of the Department of Agriculture Mike Espy, were forced to resign amidst allegations of being corrupt.

In February 1993, radical Islamists bombed the World Trade Center, which captured the nation's attention for several days. Then agents of the Bureau of Alcohol, Tobacco, and Firearms attempted to raid the Branch Davidian religious sect compound outside Waco, Texas. The sect had been founded by David Koresh. The agents had been informed that one or more members had illegal arms. Unfortunately, the attempted raid ended in a few agents and Branch Davidian members being killed.

Clinton ordered the Federal Bureau of Investigation (FBI) to take over the case. The FBI attempted to cause the Branch Davidians to surrender by shining searchlights and playing loud noises. After days of these tactics, no member had surrendered. The FBI had failed. Unfortunately, Attorney General Reno embarrassed the Clinton administration when she approved a military-style assault on the compound. As a result of the attack, the Compound caught fire. Almost 80 people, including children, were killed.

Clinton repealed rules restricting abortion counseling in federally-funded health clinics and proposed to end the ban on homosexuals in the military. Although both actions caused considerable criticism, the latter met widespread opposition from members of Congress and the leaders of the military. As a result, Clinton compromised on the latter with a "Don't ask, Don't tell" policy.

Congress passed Clinton's Omnibus Budget Reconciliation Act, which included budget cuts and tax increases intended to offset the federal deficit, in 1993. His plan to allow college students to pay off federal loans through community service was enacted as well. The Violence Against Women Act was signed into law. His nominee for the United States Supreme Court, Ruth Bader Ginsburg, gained Senate approval the same year.

Also in 1993 Clinton invited Prime Minister Yitzhak Rabin of Israel and Chairman Yassar Arafat of the Palestine Liberation Organization (PLO) to Washington, D.C., where they soon signed the Israeli-Palestinian Declaration of Principles (Oslo I Accord), which allowed Palestine to govern itself in the Gaza Strip and the West Bank.

Clinton signed the Brady Act, which required anyone interested in purchasing a handgun to have a background check by law enforcement officers, as well as the North American Free Trade Agreement (NAFTA), which had been initiated by President George H. W. Bush.

His initial handling of Haitian refugees met considerable criticism. Then in 1994 Jimmy Carter went to Haiti on behalf of the Clinton administration and several days later the military regime that had controlled the country agreed to step down. American troops were sent to the island country to assure the former president of his position as leader upon his return.

The same year the number of Democrats in the House of Representatives and the Senate of the United States decreased, causing

Clinton to become alarmed about his political future as president. Indeed, Kenneth Starr and his successor of the Office of the Independent Counsel investigated the Clintons' involvement in the Whitewater Development Corporation. After a few years, not to mention millions of dollars spent, the investigation did not prove any wrongdoing by the Clintons.

In April 1995, domestic terrorists bombed the Alfred P. Murrah Federal Building in Oklahoma City, Oklahoma, killing almost 170 people. The media covered the aftermath for days.

Before the presidential election, Clinton signed the Personal Responsibility and Work Opportunity Reconciliation Act or the Welfare Reform Act, which allowed families to receive federal aid for five years. However, determination of who received aid would be by the states, not by the federal government. The federal government would provide block grants to the states. The act also reduced spending on the Food Stamp Program.

Although Clinton and a few members of his administration faced several scandals, including financial irregularities and sexual improprieties, among others, Clinton, himself, was reelected in 1996 primarily because the economy was strong. In fact, Clinton had learned to work with Speaker of the House Newt Gingrich, a Republican, and the mostly Republican Congress. By 1998, as a result of a sound economy, Clinton and his administration were overseeing a balanced budget, a low unemployment rate, and an increase in people purchasing homes.

Unfortunately, in 1998 Kenneth Starr investigated whether Clinton had encouraged Monica Lewinsky, an intern in the White House, to lie about a possible affair. Although Clinton initially denied that an affair with Lewinsky had occurred, he eventually apologized to his family and to the American people. As a result of Starr's investigation, the House of Representatives examined the evidence and finally approved two articles of impeachment. Clinton was acquitted of the charges by the United States Senate in 1999, however.

In 1998 Clinton ordered bombs to be dropped on Iraq primarily because Iraq's government had failed to cooperate with weapons inspectors from the United Nations. A year later military forces of the North Atlantic Treaty Organization (NATO), which were led by the

United States, bombed Yugoslavia in an effort to stop the Serbians from attacking Albanians in Kosovo. Eventually, the Serbians agreed to withdraw from Kosovo.

Before he left the presidency Clinton issued numerous pardons, for which he was criticized.

After leaving the White House, he founded the William J. Clinton Foundation in 2001. Three years later the William J. Clinton Presidential Library and Museum opened in Little Rock.

Clinton's autobiography, *My Life*, was published in 2004.

* * *

From 1960 to 2000, the social climate of the United States drastically changed. While John F. Kennedy spoke about the New Frontier, Lyndon Johnson about the Great Society, Richard Nixon about Vietnam, Gerald Ford about inflation, Jimmy Carter about human rights, Ronald Reagan about conservatism, George Bush about 1,000 points of light, and Bill Clinton about rights for all, the nation was besieged with cries for equality from African-Americans and whites. This period witnessed several assassinations, countless demonstrations, peace marches, civil rights marches, sit-ins, bombings, burnings, shootings, and riots.

Certain African-Americans living in the North and South grew disillusioned with so-called civil rights legislation and justifiably so, for their apartments, houses, jobs, and schools were, for the most part, inferior to those of whites. Of course, what certain legislators attempted to do in the South, such as closing the doors of public institutions to African-Americans, merely incited vengeance. Although Dr. Martin Luther King, Jr., tried peacefully to obtain equal rights for African-Americans, his northern counterparts questioned his tactics. Before Malcom X, a former Black Muslim who had separated from the movement in 1964, was murdered in 1965, he had attempted to unite African-Americans and whites. After his murder, riots occurred in Watts, a section of Los Angeles, and more than 30 persons were killed. In 1966 Stokely Carmichael of the Student Nonviolent Coordinating Committee (SNCC) and Floyd McKissick of the Congress of Racial Equality (CORE), two militant organizations that opposed the views of Dr. Martin

Luther King, Jr.'s Southern Christian Leadership Conference, proclaimed "black power," which radicalized young African-Americans to counter their oppressors with strong-arm tactics. Riots erupted in Chicago. A year later, 1967, similar demonstrations occurred in Detroit, Newark, Atlanta, and other cities. Property damage was estimated in the millions.

The Black Panther party, which was organized in 1966 as a militant group, was chaired by Bobby Seale. Huey P. Newton and Eldridge Cleaver, who wrote in 1967 a disturbing but revealing autobiography entitled *Soul on Ice*, served as the minister of defense and as the minister of information, respectively. The party's purpose was to unite African-Americans against whites.

Other cities experienced black power as riots killed or injured people and devastated property. However, black power was not negative in every respect. Indeed, black became beautiful as the Afro became the trademark of millions.

In the latter years of the 1960s, African-Americans confronted administrators of colleges and universities. They demanded that more blacks be admitted and that more blacks be added to the faculty. They called for black studies programs. Many administrations satisfied the blacks. At some colleges and universities, however, black students took over buildings and held teach-ins to make their demands felt.

The kinds of activities on college and university campuses during the 1960s mirrored or influenced what occurred off-campus. Unlike the apathetic youth of the 1950s, the students of the 1960s reveled in President Kennedy's New Frontier. Idealism perhaps had been impressed on the young by the young president. Subsequently, students joined the Peace Corps, VISTA, or engaged in civil rights activities. They demanded their inherent right to free speech, individual or group freedom, and, of course, equality.

When President Kennedy was assassinated, idealism faded. When the war in Vietnam escalated, realism emerged, and students realized that they had to make themselves heard. In 1964 the Free Speech Movement (FSM) at the University of California, Berkeley, was the first student movement to receive national attention. Basically, the students and administration disagreed over using part of the campus to display activist material. The students confronted the administration, and the faculty voted to change the university's policy toward student speech.

The Vietnam War caused more demonstrations than perhaps free speech. Since companies such as Dow Chemical, the manufacturer of napalm, funded research on university campuses, protestors opposed the financial link between institutions of higher education and producers of weapons. The Students for a Democratic Society (SDS), a New Left group, opposed the presence of the Reserve Officers Training Corps (ROTC) on campuses. The ROTC enabled students to earn a salary and serve in one of the armed forces before they graduated from college. The SDS, through underground or alternative newspapers, encouraged mass demonstrations as well as the burning of draft cards. Some protests, particularly at the University of Wisconsin, Harvard, and Columbia University, ended in violence between the "long-haired radicals" and the police. Several students were killed and many were injured, but their efforts were witnessed by millions of television viewers and members of Congress.

Leaders of the New Left who opposed the "establishment" were harassed by the police, the FBI, or the CIA, or they were tried for violating laws. In 1968, for instance, Dr. Benjamin Spock, among others, was on trial for encouraging draft evaders to violate the Selective Service Act. A year later several leaders of the New Left were on trial for inciting a riot at the 1968 Democratic convention. Although many students marched on the Pentagon and held rallies in Washington, D. C., other students escaped reality through drugs, particularly marijuana and lysergic acid diethylamide (LSD), rock music, free sex, long hair, beads, and communes. Certain districts of cities, such as the Haight-Ashbury district of San Francisco, became havens for thousands of young people searching for their identities. Musicians, especially the Beatles and the Rolling Stones, introduced new forms of rock. Many of the songs recorded mirrored or promoted sexual promiscuity, drugs, or a new life style. Scores of film, including cycle, sex, and violence, were made for the youth market. Plays and musicals, such as *Hair*, *Jesus Christ Superstar*, and *Oh! Calcutta*, became immensely popular. Certain novelists, philosophers, poets, sociologists, and literary journalists influenced or recorded the decade. Muckraking journalists investigated various corporate, political, and social problems.

Other movements besides the peace movement appeared. These included Women's Liberation, which denounced male chauvinism and advocated equal rights, and the Gay Liberation League, which denounced societal oppression toward homosexuals and advocated equal rights. Both movements continued into the 1970s and 1980s.

Unlike the 1960s, the 1970s witnessed countless changes as a result of various groups, whether ethnic or not, making demands on legislators. Women, for instance, had a contraceptive, the pill, and legalized abortion, which enabled them to pursue their careers without having to worry about having children. No-fault divorce laws enabled marriages to dissolve with few problems. The Gray Panthers, a group formed by the elderly, demanded certain rights regarding retirement benefits. Although Congress enacted legislation that satisfied certain demands, other problems occurred as immigrants increased the nation's population by more than 400,000. People moved from one area of the country to another because of employment. Crime, particularly in cities, dramatically increased. Municipalities suffered financially. Unemployment increased. Women demanded certain rights through the National Organization for Women (NOW). African-Americans and Hispanics demanded equal rights. Indians demanded certain rights. Unfortunately, a few individuals attempted to assassinate certain political figures. Certain revolutionary groups murdered, kidnapped, burglarized, or bombed certain citizens, apartments, houses, or banks. Pornography increased in popularity.

Society had better or worse changed by 1980, since new issues had indeed forced legislators to enact new or revised laws. Although crime figures were the highest of any democratic society, innovations in the scientific community, including electronics and medicine, provided the nation with hope for tomorrow.

In the early 1980s, the country's inflation rate was almost 20 percent. Hope was merely a word to many people. Although the president and the Congress tried to alter the economy's woes, the country suffered for several years. Certain industries, such as steel and automobile, played smaller roles in the country's economy. People who had lost their jobs in manufacturing were not trained and consequently found it difficult to find employment. Newer industries, such as biotechnology and high technology, which grew during the 1980s and early 1990s, demanded a more qualified work force. People were forced to return to school and learn new skills. As a result, by the end of the 1980s, the total number of wage earners had increased, and women and minorities had been consciously preferred by employers over their white male counterparts.

During this period hundreds, if not thousands, of American family farms failed when owners could not pay toward their loans. Large-scale, heavily mechanized farms that could provide great quantities of food and other products came into existence. Change had affected every aspect of American life.

Relations with other nations improved during the 1980s and early 1990s, as more leaders discussed peace and signed treaties. This was particularly true of the Soviet Union. Mikhail Gorbachev, realizing that the Soviet Union could not compete with the United States in the arms race because of its weak economy, signed a treaty that called for the dismantling of all ground-launched U. S. and Soviet nuclear missiles. Several years later, in 1991, a group of military leaders revolted against Gorbachev. It seemed they feared his moderate proposals. The coup was quickly resolved, and soon after the countries forming the Soviet Union split. As a result, the Communist Party lost most of its power. This action helped improve relations, especially between Russia and the United States, and several other treaties regarding the reduction of nuclear weapons were signed.

When Bill Clinton became president, it seemed that most Americans had hope for a more productive life and future. However, the country was experiencing a weak economy, a major crime wave, and accelerating health costs. Although he had addressed several of these problems when he campaigned for president, one of his first acts was to end discrimination against gays in the military. Clinton received considerable criticism from military leaders, including the chairman of the Joint Chiefs of Staff, Colin Powell. Reluctantly, Clinton compromised. In addition to having nominees for attorney general withdraw over questions of ethics and major pieces of legislation blocked by the Republicans in the Senate, Clinton made another mistake, when he appointed his wife, Hillary, to chair a task force on healthcare reform. Primarily because of Republican criticism, none of the task force's recommendations were ever submitted to Congress.

Clinton did achieve some success, however, when Congress passed the North American Free Trade Agreement. He enjoyed further success when Congress enacted legislation to reverse the nation's debt. He also signed into law the Family and Medical Leave Act and the Brady Handgun Violence Prevention Act.

In 1993 terrorists attacked the World Trade Center in New York City.

A year later Republicans won a majority in both houses of Congress, and Clinton compromised by supporting stronger legislation that addressed the nation's debt as well as the nation's welfare system. However, Kenneth Starr began investigating the president and his wife's business dealings in Arkansas. Known as Whitewater, the investigation lasted several years and cost the country millions of dollars. Starr found no conclusive evidence that the Clintons had done anything wrong.

In 1995 Timothy McVeigh detonated a bomb in Oklahoma City that destroyed the Alfred P. Murrah Federal Building and killed more than 168 people. More than 500 were injured. Americans were stunned by this act of violence.

A year later, primarily because of Clinton's optimism and the country's economy, American voters went to the polls and voted for him a second time. However, Starr was allowed to expand his investigation. Later, he uncovered evidence that the president had been seeing Monica Lewinsky, a White House intern. For months, Clinton denied that he had an affair with Monica. Eventually, he acknowledged having the affair and apologized to the American public. The House of Representatives conducted hearings, and Clinton was impeached for perjury and obstruction of justice. In 1999, however, he was acquitted of the charges by the Senate.

Clinton was damaged, but Americans approved of the job he was doing primarily because of the economy. Indeed, his administration was responsible for the first balanced budget and budget surplus since the late 1960s. Unemployment was extremely low. As a result, many Americans purchased homes. The stock market was high, which reflected Americans' confidence in the economy.

During the Clinton years, Iraq's government, which had agreed to long-term monitoring of its weapons programs by the United Nations, clashed with inspectors and refused to comply with the agreements. In 1998 air strikes against Iraq's weapons facilities were ordered by the United States and the United Kingdom.

Notes:

1. The founders had no intention for the federal government to adopt socialism. Yet, during the 1900s, the federal government became more socialistic as a result of specific legislation being signed by presidents. The initial source for these socialistic programs was the federal income tax that was enacted in the early 1900s. As more socialistic programs came into existence, additional taxes were enacted. The first major socialistic program was Social Security, which was enacted by President Franklin Delano Roosevelt. President Lyndon B. Johnson enacted Medicare and Medicaid. He also enacted other socialistic programs that helped the poor. President Barack Obama enacted another, Obamacare. Together, these socialistic programs are expensive and have caused the nation's national debt to increase every year. Without question, the founders had no intention for the federal government to enact such socialistic programs. Consequently, they would be opposed to the federal government adopting socialism.
2. No so-called superpower nation should ever find itself needing an essential product from a foreign country, especially a foreign country that has a different political philosophy. This is the result of one or more individuals who are ignorant being allowed to make such decisions. Or the individuals responsible for such decisions accepted bribes.

References:

Alter, Jonathan. *His Very Best: Jimmy Carter, a Life*. New York: Simon & Schuster, 2020.

Ambrose, Stephen A. *Nixon, Vol. 3: Ruin and Recovery, 1973-1990*. New York: Simon & Schuster, 1991.

Ambrose, Stephen A. *Nixon, Vol. 2: The Triumph of a Politician, 1962-1972*. New York: Simon & Schuster, 1989.

Beschloss, Michael. *The Crisis Years: Kennedy and Khruschev, 1960-63*. New York: Harper Collins, 1991.

Brands, H. W. *Reagan: The Life*. New York: Doubleday, 2015.

Califano, Jr., Joseph A. *The Triumph and Tragedy of Lyndon Johnson: The White House Years*. New York: Simon & Schuster, 1991.

Cannon, James. *Gerald R. Ford: An Honorable Life. Afterword by Scott Cannon*. Ann Arbor: University of Michigan Press, 2013.

Cannon, Lou. *President Reagan: The Role of a Lifetime*. New York: Public Affairs, 2000.

Caro, Robert A. *The Passage of Power: The Years of Lyndon Johnson*. New York: Knopf, 2012.

Dallek, Robert. *An Unfinished Life: John F. Kennedy, 1917-1963*. New York: Little, Brown and Co., 2003.

Dallek, Robert. *Lyndon B. Johnson: Portrait of a President*. New York: Oxford University Press, 2005.

Drew, Elizabeth. *On the Edge: the Clinton Presidency*. New York: Simon & Schuster, 1995.

Eizenstat, Stuart E. *President Carter: The White House Years. Foreword by Madeleine Albright*. New York: Thomas Dunne Books, 2018.

Engel, Jeffrey A. *When the World Seemed New: George H. W. Bush and the End of the Cold War*. Boston: Houghton Mifflin Harcourt, 2017.

Farrell, John A. *Richard Nixon: The Life*. New York: Doubleday, 2017.

Giglio, James. *The Presidency of John F. Kennedy*. Lawrence: University Press of Kansas, 1991.

Green, Fitzhugh. *George Bush: an Intimate Portrait*. New York: Hippocrene Books, 1989.

Greene, John R. *The Presidency of George Bush*, 2nd ed. Lawrence: University Press of Kansas, 2015.

Hamilton, Nigel. *JFK: Reckless Youth* New York: Random House, 1992.

Hargrove, Erwin C. *Jimmy Carter as President: Leadership and the Politics of the Public Good*. Baton Rouge: Louisiana State University Press, 1988.

Harris, John F. *The Survivor: Bill Clinton in the White House*. New York: Random House, 2005.

Hayward, Steven F. *The Age of Reagan: The Conservative Counterrevolution: 1980-1989*. New York: Crown Forum, 2009.

Kaufman, Scott. *Ambition, Pragmatism, and Party: A Political Biography of Gerald R. Ford*. Lawrence: University Press of Kansas, 2017.

Maney, Patrick J. *Bill Clinton: New Gilded Age President*. Lawrence: University Press of Kansas, 2016.

Maraniss, David. *First in His Class: A Biography of Bill Clinton*. New York: Simon & Schuster, 1995.

Meacham, Jon. *Destiny and Power: The American Odyssey of George Herbert Walker Bush*. New York: Random House, 2015.

Parmet, Herbert S. *George Bush: The Life of a Lone Star Yankee*. New York: Scribner's Sons, 1997.

Reeves, Richard. *A Ford, Not a Lincoln*. New York: Harcourt Brace Jovanovich, 1975.

Reeves, Thomas C. *A Question of Character: A Life of John F. Kennedy*. London: Arrow Books, 1992.

Schlesinger, Arthur M. *A Thousand Days: JFK in the White House*. Boston: Houghton Mifflin, 1965.

Spitz, Bob. *Reagan: An American Journey*. New York: Penguin Press, 2018.

Unger, Irwin and Debi Unger. *LBJ: A Life*. Hoboken, N. J.: Wiley, 1999.

Chapter 6

Political and Social Change in the United States, from 2001 to 2020

George W. Bush was the oldest child of President George H. W. Bush and First Lady Barbara Bush. He grew up primarily in Midland and Houston, Texas. In the early 1960s, he attended Phillips Academy in Andover, Massachusetts. Later, he attended Yale University, from which he graduated in 1968.

Bush became an officer in the Texas Air National Guard, from which he was discharged in 1973, and then attended Harvard Business School, from which he graduated in 1975. He returned to Midland, Texas, and eventually founded an oil and gas company. In 1977 he married Laura Welch, a teacher, with whom he had fraternal twin daughters.

Although he ran for Congress in 1978, he was not successful. In 1986 he sold his company and worked on his father's presidential campaign in Washington, D. C. After the election, he moved to Dallas. Along with other investors, he purchased the Texas Rangers baseball team.

Bush ran against Ann Richards, the Democratic governor of Texas, in 1994. The press published negative stories about his business transactions, especially about his selling of stock in 1990, during the campaign, but Bush easily defeated Richards.

As governor, he immediately increased spending on public education and instituted tougher laws concerning crime. He was reelected in a landslide in 1998. A year later he announced he intended to run for president of the United States. On the campaign trail, a few reporters asked about his consumption of liquor, which, he claimed, he had stopped drinking when he turned 40 years old.

Bush became the Republican nominee.

Al Gore, who served as vice president under President Clinton, was the Democratic nominee. Both candidates ran successful campaigns. In fact, Al Gore, who won the popular vote, asked for a manual recount in several counties in Florida. Eventually, Florida's Supreme Court ordered that a manual recount of the more than 40,000 questionable votes be made. However, the United States Supreme Court soon overturned Florida's Supreme Court order. Consequently, the electoral votes went to George W. Bush.

Besides John Quincy Adams, the son of President John Adams, Bush was only the second child of a president to be elected to the office.

President Bush immediately reinstated a ban on aid to international groups that performed or even counseled abortions. The ban had been initiated by President Ronald Reagan but had been lifted by President Bill Clinton. He also created the Office of Faith-Based and Community Initiatives in the White House. This office served to ease regulations on religious charities and related organizations in an effort to help the poor and disadvantaged. Of course, certain members of Congress and the press criticized the president for bringing what they perceived to be a religious-based office into the White House.

In February 2001, Bush proposed a massive tax cut of more than one trillion dollars that eventually was approved by Congress and signed into law in June.

The Bush administration refused to ratify the Kyoto Protocol, which was the agreement that had imposed emission limits on gases responsible for global warming, primarily because the agreement had not applied to developing nations.

Unfortunately, in September 2001, the administration's attention turned from domestic policies to foreign policies, when four commercial airplanes were skyjacked by Islamist terrorists. Two of the planes destroyed the World Trade Center buildings in New York City, one destroyed part of the Pentagon building in Washington, D. C., and one crashed in a field in Pennsylvania. As a result of the crashes and the destruction of the buildings, several thousand people were killed.

The Bush administration realized that Osama Bin Laden and his terrorist organization, Al-Qaeda, were responsible for the attacks. In response, coalition military forces initiated Operation Enduring Freedom against the Taliban in Afghanistan. According to the administration, the Taliban had allowed Bin Laden and his group of terrorists to live in the country. The administration proposed the Uniting and Strengthening America by Providing Appropriate Tools Required to Intercept and Obstruct Terrorism Act (PATRIOT Act), which allowed the Federal Bureau of Investigation (FBI), among other law-enforcement agencies, to basically spy on individuals who had connections to other individuals or groups that were considered suspect. This act was passed by Congress and signed by President Bush.

Beginning in 2002, if individuals captured in Afghanistan were determined to be members of Al-Qaeda, they were shipped to a prison at Guantanamo Bay, Cuba. This practice was criticized when the press learned that the prisoners were being held without charge and with no legal representation. Of course, the prisoners were believed to be members of a terrorist organization, not a legitimate representative body of a recognized nation at war. In short, articles relating to the Geneva Conventions did not apply, according to the administration.[1]

Without question, the administration was concerned with terrorism. However, President Bush did not neglect domestic problems. For instance, in 2002 he signed the No Child Left Behind Act, which basically changed the curriculum in American public schools. Indeed, each state was required to test students each year to determine each child's progress in the classroom. Teachers were required to meet higher standards in order to be certified. Of course, certain members of Congress and the press criticized the bill, claiming it was unconstitutional primarily because it enabled the federal government to control public education. According to these critics, public education was supposed to be controlled by the states. The same critics also complained that the federal government had not provided enough funds to implement the requirements.

In 2002 the National Security Agency (NSA) was authorized to scrutinize e-mails and international telephone calls made by Americans and others from the United States. Although the authorization was debated by certain members of Congress as well as by members of the press, Congress eventually passed legislation that allowed such activity to continue.

President Bush was concerned with protecting Americans at home. For this purpose, his administration created the Department of Homeland Security. Bush appointed Tom Ridge, the governor of Pennsylvania, to manage it.

In 2002 President Bush and President Vladimir Putin of Russia signed a nuclear arms treaty in Moscow that reduced each nation's nuclear arsenal by two-thirds.

Later the same year President Bush addressed the Security Council of the United Nations. He insisted that Saddam Hussein's government had weapons of mass destruction and that the Security Council needed to develop a resolution so weapons inspectors could return to Iraq. Several months later President Bush addressed the Security Council again, stating the body needed to enforce the resolutions in Iraq.

In October 2002, the Congress of the United States authorized President Bush to use military force, if necessary, against Iraq.

In 2003 the Columbia space shuttle exploded, killing all seven crew members aboard. The nation followed the press coverage for weeks.

Although the space shuttle was on everyone's mind, including those inside the Bush administration, Afghanistan and Iraq were discussed as well. In fact, President Bush had claimed Iraq's government had tried to purchase enriched uranium primarily for nuclear weapons. In March he informed Saddam Hussein that he and his family had 48 hours to leave Iraq or face the consequences. Hussein refused to leave. President Bush ordered Operation Iraqi Freedom, which was a military invasion. The Iraq War, which was fought mainly by the United States and Great Britain, forced Saddam Hussein from power. However, no weapons of mass destruction were found. According to the federal government, evidence indicated that Hussein had been interested in producing such weapons whenever the sanctions by the United Nations were lifted.

President Bush had thought the war would be brief, which it was, but the country was unstable as a result. Consequently, in order to bring stability to the country, a new government had to be established. President Bush ordered more than 100,000 American soldiers to remain in Iraq. Unfortunately, the occupation was expensive. In addition to costing several billion dollars a month, numerous American soldiers were killed or injured.

As if the country's involvement in Iraq was not grave enough, President Bush criticized the government of Iran for its interest in nuclear energy, especially its interest in nuclear weapons. Primarily because of President Bush's criticism, several members of the press wondered if he was considering a military operation in Iran.

Besides a major military operation abroad, the Bush administration was forced to deal with a weak economy at home. In 2003 President Bush persuaded Congress to pass a second major bill that cut taxes amounting to several hundred billion dollars. Hopefully, the tax cuts would help strengthen the economy.

In addition, he reformed Medicare, the health insurance program for seniors, when he signed the Medicare Modernization Act (MMA) the same year. The bill allowed those enrolled in Medicare to obtain coverage for prescription drugs through private insurance companies. The bill also allowed more private insurance plans for medical services to be available to enrollees. Of course, certain members of Congress criticized this act before it was passed.

The same year President Bush proposed an Emergency Plan for AIDs Relief that would cost $15 billion over a five-year period. The plan, which was approved by Congress, provided medicines and care to millions of victims of HIV/AIDs.

Although President Bush had discussed the concept months earlier, finally, in 2004, the administration received authorization from Congress to establish the Millennium Challenge Corporation primarily for the purpose of helping poor countries that were committed to democracy. The corporation approved grants that helped reduce poverty and stimulated the economy of certain countries.

The same year certain members of the press learned that captives, particularly those being held in prisons like Abu Ghraib, which was outside the country, had been subjected to water boarding and other questionable techniques primarily for the purpose of gaining information. These journalists accused the administration of using torture. This accusation was unfounded, however, according to the Bush administration.[2]

In 2004 George Tenet, the director of the Central Intelligence Agency (CIA), resigned. Later the same year Senator John Kerry, a Democrat, opposed President Bush in the presidential election. However, Bush won the popular and electoral votes. In addition, the Republicans increased their majorities in the House of Representatives and the United States Senate. After the election, Secretary of State Colin Powell resigned. President Bush appointed Condoleezza Rice to the position.

In 2005, according to public opinion polls, most Americans were opposed to America's involvement in Iraq. In fact, most Americans thought the war had been a mistake. Needless to say, President Bush's popularity, which had been very high months before, declined.

In 2005 Congress passed the Omnibus Energy bill that the Bush administration had proposed. The bill supported traditional energy companies that produced oil and natural gas. The bill also provided incentives for the use of alternative sources of energy such as solar and wind.

When the Gulf coast was hammered by Hurricane Katrina in 2005, the levee system in New Orleans broke, causing massive flooding of the city. Unfortunately, the Bush administration was severely criticized for its inadequate response to the storm's destruction.

On the other hand, President Bush received some satisfaction when his nominee for Chief Justice of the United States Supreme Court, John Roberts, was confirmed by the United States Senate weeks later.

In response to the negative press coverage of how captives were treated in prisons as well as pressure from numerous constituents, Congress passed the Detainee Treatment Act, which basically banned water boarding and other so-called "torture" techniques of prisoners by the military. President Bush signed the legislation in late 2005.

In early 2006, President Bush's nominee for a justice of the United States Supreme Court, Samuel Alito, Jr., was confirmed by the United States Senate.

The same year Congress passed the Military Commissions Act, which was in response to the decision by the United States Supreme Court in the case *Hamden v. Rumsfeld*. The justices had determined that the tactics used on certain prisoners at Guantanamo Bay were in violation of the Geneva Conventions and the Uniform Code of Military Justice. The act prevented prisoners who were not citizens of the United States from challenging their predicament in the federal courts.

Later, in 2006, President Bush signed the bill that provided funding for a 700-mile fence along the border between the United States and Mexico.

In 2007 I. Lewis "Scooter" Libby, Vice President Dick Cheney's chief of staff, was convicted on charges of perjury and obstruction of justice in relation to the investigation of who leaked the identity of a Central Intelligence Agency (CIA) operative in 2003. Libby was not accused of disclosing the name, however. President Bush commuted Libby's prison sentence in 2007. President Trump pardoned Libby in 2018.

The same year President Bush signed legislation that stipulated automobiles had to be more fuel efficient by 2020.

In 2008, in an effort to stimulate the economy, which was extremely weak, Bush proposed a stimulus package that provided individuals with several hundred dollars, rebates for families with children, and tax deductions for businesses. Soon Congress passed the Emergency Economic Stabilization Act.

Although he had vetoed a farm bill costing several hundred billion dollars, Congress overrode his veto. As a result, the bill provided $300 billion of subsidies to farmers as well as to the Food Stamp program.

In September 2008, Fannie Mae (Federal National Mortgage Association) and Freddie Mac (Federal Home Loan Mortgage

Corporation) were placed under the control of the United States Treasury in an effort to prevent either from failing.

Before he left office, President Bush bailed out the banking sector by signing legislation that provided several hundred billion dollars. Primarily because General Motors and Chrysler faced possible bankruptcy, he bailed out both by signing legislation that provided several billion dollars to each.

Although John McCain ran for the presidency in 2008, he was defeated by Barack Obama, the first African-American to be elected president of the United States..

When President Bush left office, he and his wife moved to Dallas, Texas. In 2009 the George W. Bush Presidential Center opened on the campus of Southern Methodist University.

In 2010 Bush published *Decision Points*, which concerned his years as president. In 2014 he published *41: A Portrait of My Father*, which was a biography of George H. W. Bush, the former president.

Bush also painted portraits of various individuals, including veterans. Many of these portraits appeared in *Portraits of Courage: A Commander in Chief's Tribute to America's Warriors*, which was published in 2017.

Barack Hussein Obama was born in Hawaii. His father was from Kenya and his mother was from Kansas; they had met while attending the University of Hawaii. Although they married, the marriage ended in divorce when Barack was two years old. In 1967 his mother remarried and the family moved to Indonesia.

Obama lived in Indonesia until he returned to Hawaii in 1971 to live with his maternal grandparents and to attend the Punahou School, from which he graduated several years later. He attended Occidental College in Los Angeles. Then, after two years, he transferred to Columbia University in New York City, from which he graduated in 1983.

Obama worked in New York City until 1985. He moved to Chicago, where he worked for a community development organization. In 1988 he attended Harvard Law School, from which he graduated in

1991. As a student, Obama served as the president of the *Harvard Law Review*.

Before he earned his law degree, Obama worked as an associate at a law firm in Chicago. There, he met Michelle Robinson. After he had gained employment as a lawyer, he and Michelle married in 1992.

Obama wrote *Dreams From My Father: A Story of Race and Inheritance*, which explored his father's family and was published in 1995, the year he campaigned for the Illinois Senate. He won in 1996. Several years later he ran for the United States Senate. He won in 2004.

Similar to running for a higher position after serving a few years in the Illinois Senate, Obama campaigned for president a few years after becoming a senator of the United States. Although Senator Hillary Clinton was the leading member of the Democratic Party who was campaigning for president, Obama eventually became the party's nominee. He chose Senator Joseph Biden as his running mate.

Senator John McCain, a well-known member of Congress who had been held a prisoner during the Vietnam War, was nominated for president by the Republicans. He chose Sarah Palin, the governor of Alaska, as his running mate.

The American people voted for Obama, the first African-American to be elected president of the United States. Immediately, President Obama signed the Lilly Ledbetter Fair Pay Act, which addressed the gap in wages between men and women. However, this was a minor problem compared to the overall weak economy, which grew worse every day and effected everyone. In response to it, Obama signed the American Recovery and Reinvestment Act, which provided more than $700 billion for every sector that made up the country's overall economy. The stimulus bill included tax cuts and unemployment benefits as well.

He also provided help for the financial and automobile industries. However, unlike the previous administration, which had opposed the government funding stem-cell research, Obama approved it.

During the first summer of his administration, President Obama nominated Sonia Sotomayor as a justice of the United States Supreme

Court. Sotomayor was confirmed by the United States Senate and was the first Hispanic to serve as a justice on the court.

In October 2009, Obama received the Nobel Peace Prize. Many people who worked in the federal government questioned the committee's decision primarily because Obama had just become president and had not done anything worthy enough for the prize. Of course, the committee may have given the prize to President Obama because he was the first African-American to become a president of the United States.

Although Obama and members of his administration had hoped the economic stimulus bill would create several million jobs within a few years, the unemployment rate increased to more than 10 percent in 2009. Apparently, the bill was not working—yet.

Obama put the poor economy temporarily out of his mind while he focused on one of his presidential campaign promises—healthcare reform, which he soon proposed. Obama believed Americans needed to have health insurance either through their employers or through the federal government. Although Republican members of both houses of Congress opposed such legislation and consequently argued with their Democratic colleagues, the Democrats, without Republican support, eventually passed the health insurance reform bill, which Obama signed into law in 2010. The Patient Protection and Affordable Care Act (PPACA), which soon became known as Obamacare, expanded Medicaid coverage. In order to help small businesses with healthcare expenses, the bill provided tax credits. The bill also prevented insurance companies from refusing to insure patients with medical conditions.

Before the bill was passed and signed, however, President Obama had told the American people that if they were happy with their healthcare insurance, they could keep it. He also told them they could keep their primary care doctors. Unfortunately, when the bill became law, many individuals learned they could not keep their primary care doctors. In fact, when the health insurance exchanges came into existence to help people secure health insurance, those who did not have health insurance had to select plans that were offered. Many of these plans had restrictions similar to Medicare Advantage plans. In short, the plans listed specific doctors for subscribers. As if this was not bad enough, when the federal website for health insurance appeared online, it failed numerous times for several months. Critics wondered if the health policies being sold would be like the website—filled with problems. To say the least, President Obama and members of his administration were embarrassed.

In April 2010, President Obama and President Medvedev of Russia signed the Strategic Arms Reduction Treaty (START), which reduced the number of nuclear weapons in each country.

A few days later Deepwater Horizon, an oil rig off the coast of Louisiana, exploded and killed 11 people and injured several others. According to the federal government, the explosion also caused more than 200,000,000 gallons of oil to pour into the Gulf of Mexico, which was one of the worst environmental disasters in the country's history.

As if this disaster was not grave enough, another one happened the same month. Twenty-nine coal miners were killed in an explosion in West Virginia.

Although the administration was concerned with both events, President Obama found time to nominate Elena Kagan as a justice of the United States Supreme Court. Kagan was confirmed by the United States Senate.

In July 2010, President Obama signed the Dodd-Frank Wall Street Reform and Consumer Protection Act, which, hopefully, would end the massive taxpayer-funded bailouts of large financial institutions by giving regulators the authority to break up large unwieldy companies and corporations that had problems. The bill also protected consumers whenever they sought a loan or obtained a credit card.

In October 2010, President Obama signed the 21st Century Communication and Video Accessibility Act, which provided Americans who were blind, deaf, or had a visual impairment equal access to new technology.

Before 2011, Americans went to the polls and voted for more Republicans to serve in the House of Representatives primarily because they were not happy about the economy. Indeed, not only was unemployment still high, but sales of houses were declining. In short, at least to the American voter, the Democrats had failed to turn the country around.

In December 2010, President Obama signed the Healthy, Hunger-Free Kids Act, which provided funds for free lunch programs in public schools. He also signed the Tax Relief, Unemployment Insurance Reauthorization, and Job Creation Act, which extended the tax cuts and unemployment benefits for many Americans. The bill had been instituted by President George W. Bush. President Obama signed the act primarily because the Republicans were the majority in the House of Representatives. He also signed a bill that ended the "Don't ask, Don't tell" policy for the military, which had banned openly homosexual people from serving in the United States Armed Forces.

In January 2011, in Tucson, Arizona, a man with a weapon shot 19 people. Six were killed. Representative Gabrielle Giffords was shot in the head, but she survived.

In May 2011, President Obama informed the American people that Osama Bin Laden, the leader of Al-Qaeda, a terrorist organization, had been killed by a team of Navy Seals. Finally, after several years, the person behind the worst terrorist attack on American soil had been killed.

After much discussion, Congress passed the Budget Control Act, which raised the federal debt ceiling and which President Obama signed into law in August 2011. Two months later he announced that the country's role in the war in Iraq was over. However, along with several other countries, the United States provided soldiers to protect people in Libya after violence erupted primarily because Muammar al-Qaddafi, the leader of the country, would not step down or leave. Later, military planes bombed Libyan government installations. Within a few months most of Libya was controlled by rebels. Although Qaddafi tried to hide, he was soon killed in Surt.

In February 2012, the administration froze the assets of the Iranian government that were in the United States primarily because the Iranian government had engaged in "deceptive practices" regarding its nuclear program.

A few months later President Obama signed the Stop Trading on Congressional Knowledge Act (STOCK), which sought to eliminate insider trading, especially among those who served in Congress.

During the summer of 2012 President Obama initiated a new policy regarding immigration. Basically, the policy allowed undocumented immigrants who came to the country as children to remain if they lived in the country for five years, had no criminal record, earned a diploma from a high school in the United States, or served in the United States Armed Forces. Any undocumented immigrant who met these conditions could apply for a two-year work permit, which could be renewed. Although the policy addressed another major problem, it was severely criticized by Republicans in Congress. Some members believed the policy was too lenient. Others pointed out that the parents of these children had broken the law by entering the country illegally; consequently, the children should not necessarily be rewarded. Still, others believed the children were breaking the law every day they remained in the country.

In August 2012, the administration released new standards for automobile fuel efficiency. As a result, cars and light trucks in the United States had to average 55 miles per gallon of gasoline by 2025.

In 2012 the economy slightly improved. The unemployment rate was below nine percent in January and below eight percent in September.

In September 2012, terrorists attacked a United States installation in Benghazi, Libya, and killed the ambassador and a few other Americans. The administration was criticized for doing little, if anything, to protect these people. In fact, certain media outlets covered the story for weeks, if not months.

In October 2012, Hurricane Sandy, which struck the eastern United States, especially New Jersey and New York City, killed more than 100 people and left millions of homes without power. Communities and towns along the coast were severely damaged.

Although President Obama, like leaders of other countries, called for President Bashar al-Assad of Syria to step down primarily because he had killed thousands of protestors who were opposed to his government, President Bashar remained in power. As a result, President Obama increased economic sanctions against Syria. He increased economic sanctions against Iran because the country was interested in producing nuclear weapons.

President Obama and Vice President Biden were re-nominated at the Democratic National Convention. Mitt Romney, a former governor of Massachusetts, and Paul Ryan, representative of Wisconsin, were nominated by the Republicans. Romney should have defeated President Obama primarily because of the sluggish economy, not to mention the problems abroad. However, he displayed weakness during one of the debates and consequently failed to impress enough voters to win.

In December 2012, a young man with a weapon entered Sandy Hook Elementary School in Newtown, Connecticut, and killed 20 children and six employees before he killed himself. Through executive action, President Obama attempted to improve school safety by making certain that individuals were checked out thoroughly before they could purchase firearms.

In 2013 President Obama appointed John Kerry, a senator from Massachusetts, as Secretary of State Hillary Clinton's successor. Kerry was confirmed by the United States Senate. Chuck Hagel succeeded Leon Panetta as secretary of defense and Jack Lew succeeded Timothy Geithner as secretary of the treasury.

In January 2013, President Obama signed the American Taxpayer Relief Act, which extended tax cuts for many Americans and limited tax deductions for those who earned more than $400,000 per year. The act also extended unemployment benefits and increased payroll tax rates.

Although Obama discussed the Keystone XL Pipeline with officials from Canada in 2013, eventually he rejected the proposal.

In March 2013, President Obama signed the Violence Against Women Reauthorization Act, which provided additional protection for women by improving law enforcement techniques. The act also improved services for female victims of violent crimes.

Unfortunately, an act of terrorism occurred again in the United States, when homemade bombs exploded during the Boston Marathon.

At least three people were killed and several hundred were injured. One terrorist suspect was killed while the other was captured.

As if the intentional bombing was not grave enough, a fertilizer plant in Texas caught fire and exploded, killing 15 and injuring several hundred people. President Obama addressed the nation, but his words were hollow to many people. Indeed, these people thought there were many questions that needed to be answered by the administration.

On the other hand, the country's economy was improving slightly. For instance, the unemployment rate was under eight percent in July. By the end of the year, the rate was under seven percent.

In February 2014, President Obama signed the Federal Agriculture Reform and Risk Management Act, which provided almost a trillion dollars for nutritional and agricultural programs in the United States for four years. The same month he signed an executive order that increased the minimum wage for all workers on federal contracts.

Although the unemployment figure and President Obama's actions were positive, the administration was severely criticized after the public learned the National Security Agency (NSA), an agency within the United States Department of Defense, was monitoring the telephone calls as well as the internet activities of individuals who may be linked to possible terrorists or terrorist organizations. Additional criticism came from specific members of the press when executives of news organizations learned that officials from the Justice Department had obtained records of editors and reporters.[3]

Unfortunately, criticism of the administration would not stop. When the House of Representatives of the United States held hearings about the attack in Benghazi, Libya, in 2014, the president and the administration were criticized again, especially by Republicans.

Other criticism was aimed at the administration when it was learned that veterans had to wait weeks, if not months, for medical care in facilities run by the Department of Veterans Affairs. As a result, the secretary of the Department of Veterans Affairs resigned in 2014.

In the 2014 midterm elections, Republicans increased their majority in the House of Representatives and gained control of the United States Senate.

In February 2015, President Obama signed the Clay Hunt Suicide Prevention for American Veterans Act, which was to raise awareness of the problem and provide help to veterans.

During the summer of 2015, President Obama addressed climate change by limiting carbon emissions from power plants. Later, in November 2015, he attended the United Nations Climate Change Conference in Paris, France, and signed an agreement that limited emissions.

Unfortunately, during the summer of 2015, a man with a weapon entered a nightclub that was frequented by homosexuals and killed almost 50 people. He also injured more than 50 people before he was killed by police. Purportedly, the man was a terrorist who hated homosexuals.

President Obama nominated Merrick Garland as a justice of the United States Supreme Court after Associate Justice Antonin Scalia died, but the Republicans in the United States Senate refused to consider the nominee.

Although President Obama supported Hillary Clinton for president, she lost to Donald Trump, the Republican candidate, in 2016.

The administration received additional criticism primarily because President Obama made several decisions that were not popular. For instance, his administration exchanged five Taliban prisoners for captured United States Army Sergeant Bowe Bergdahl in 2014. Many Republicans serving in Congress believed the administration had given too much for Bergdahl's release.

When President Obama attempted to normalize relations with Cuba in 2014, many Republicans criticized him for it. When members of the press wrote about it, many people from Cuba who lived in Florida expressed their unhappiness. After all, they remembered what had been done to members of their families.

In addition, the administration provided economic and military aid to Egypt's military government in 2015. When violence broke out in Egypt, many Republicans believed the administration should have withdrawn aid. However, the administration did not.

When the administration reached an agreement with Iran over its nuclear program in 2016, many Republicans questioned the agreement. They also criticized the administration when it gave money to the Iranian government.

After he left office, President Obama and his family settled in Washington, D.C. In addition to starting a production company, both Michelle and Barack wrote popular books about their lives.

Donald John Trump was born in New York City. His father, Frederick Trump, was a successful builder of family houses in Queens, a borough of New York City. When Donald was a teenager, his parents sent him to the New York Military Academy in Cornwall-on-Hudson, New York, where he became a member of the baseball team. Donald graduated in 1964 and then enrolled at Fordham University in New York City. Two years later he transferred to the University of Pennsylvania's Wharton School, where he majored in economics. He graduated in 1968.

Trump joined his father's business the same year. In the early 1970s, the Department of Justice of the United States filed a suit against the Trump Management Corporation because of its discrimination against African-Americans in its rental policy. As a result, the company changed the policy.

By the mid-1970s, Trump was featured in the media primarily because of his acumen as a successful businessman as well as his interest in dating fashion models. Indeed, he met Ivana Winklmayr, a model, who had been born in Czechoslovakia, in 1976. A year later they married and had three children. The couple was married until 1991.

Two years later Trump married Marla Maples, an actress, with whom he had another child. However, they divorced in 1999. Trump met Melania Knauss, a model, before his divorce from Maples was final. Knauss had been born in Yugoslavia. They eventually married in 2005 and had one child.

Trump had become head of his father's company in the early 1970s and had changed the name to the Trump Organization. Instead of building houses, however, he focused on building properties in Manhattan, another borough of New York City. In fact, he built major properties or renovated buildings, including the Grand Hyatt Hotel, the

Trump Tower, and the Plaza Hotel, among others. He also built or renovated major properties in other cities, states, and countries. His company opened casinos and golf courses, too. In addition, the company sold Trump-related merchandise. However, Trump did not restrict his interest to skyscrapers, hotels, casinos, golf courses, or merchandise. In 2004, for instance, he founded Trump University, a real-estate educational program that eventually faced a lawsuit. Although the program's courses included well-written textbooks, Trump closed the business in 2010.

Trump's other business interests included a football team, the Miss Universe Organization, and the popular "The Apprentice" series on television.

His primary business, the Trump Organization, has filed for bankruptcy several times over the years. However, Trump has never filed for bankruptcy for himself.

As if the above did not require all of his time, Trump actually wrote or co-wrote several popular books over the years, including the bestselling *Trump: The Art of the Deal*, which was published in 1987, and *Trump: The Art of the Comeback*, which was published in 1997.

In June 2015, he announced that he was running for president of the United States. Although he had monetarily supported both Democrats and Republicans over the years, he ran as a Republican. Trump had to defeat numerous Republican candidates, including Jeb Bush, the former governor of Florida and the younger brother of President George W. Bush as well as the son of President George H. W. Bush, Scott Walker, the governor of Wisconsin, Ted Cruz, a senator from Texas, Marco Rubio, a senator from Florida, and John Kasich, the governor of Ohio, among others.

Celebrities and members of the press dismissed Trump as a serious candidate, but his campaign, which focused on making the country great again, resonated with millions of Americans who had grown frustrated with politicians who seemed to be in the pockets of foreign and domestic lobbyists in the sense that every major bill passed by Congress gave millions or billions of taxpayer dollars to other countries and special interests, including organizations that were not part of the federal government. In short, Trump persevered by realizing that many Americans had grown tired of both parties promising this and that and not delivering. Trump also realized that Americans were paying taxes that should be used for the United States and its debts, not for other countries and special interests. In essence, he pressed the right buttons and consequently became the Republican Party's nominee.[4]

However, Trump faced the Democratic Party's nominee, Hillary Clinton, who had served in President Obama's administration. Before that she had served as a senator from New York. Although she had been expected to win the election, she did not win the electoral college. As a result, Trump became president.

Immediately, as if members of the press had a vested interest in the outcome of the presidential election, they criticized Trump when he ran for the office and especially after he won. In fact, members of the American media were relentless in their criticism throughout his term in office. Primarily because the American media was hostile to him and his administration, no matter what he and his administration accomplished, President Trump believed he had to present his messages to his constituents through social media, including Twitter, which he did on a regular basis. Not only did he have to deal with biased reporters, he had to deal with employees of the federal government who were against him. In fact, several attempted to undermine his administration by leaking information to members of the American press and/or to certain members of Congress.

After he entered the White House as president, Trump held several rallies primarily to show his appreciation to his constituents for supporting him. He filled cabinet positions with qualified individuals, several of whom were not politicians. However, several members grew tired of working for President Trump or were asked to resign or were fired for various reasons. Since Trump was described as a workaholic by those who knew him, few members of his cabinet could keep up with him.[5]

In January 2017, President Trump restricted travel for individuals from certain Muslim countries as a result of possible terrorist activities. As if they did not realize the possible danger, one or more federal judges blocked Trump's order primarily because of how the order had been phrased. Soon, lawyers inside the Justice Department developed restrictions that satisfied the court's concerns, and the travel ban went into effect in June 2017. Unfortunately, numerous travelers were allowed into the country as a result of the United States Supreme Court upholding a federal judge's order.[6]

President Trump also informed the governments of the relevant countries that the United States was withdrawing from the Trans-Pacific Partnership, which basically was a free trade deal. Trump opposed the deal primarily because it did not necessarily benefit the United States as much as he thought it should.

President Trump received considerable criticism when he transferred the control of his company to his older sons and promised the company would not conduct any new business with foreign countries or with the government of the United States. In fact, he faced more than one lawsuit because of the domestic and foreign emoluments clauses of the constitution. The domestic clause prohibits a president from receiving any emolument from the federal government or the states above his compensation. The foreign clause prohibits federal officeholders from accepting gifts, payments, or other items of value from anyone representing a foreign government without congressional approval. As a result of not placing the company in a blind trust, Trump was sued by the attorney general of Maryland and Democratic members of Congress, among others. These suits claimed the president had violated the emoluments clauses.[7]

Before February 2017, President Trump nominated Neil Gorsuch as a justice of the United States Supreme Court. Gorsuch was confirmed by the United States Senate in April 2017. Although Gorsuch did not experience a difficult confirmation, Brett Kavanaugh, who was nominated a year later, did. In fact, several senators revealed their political biases on television.[8]

Retired Army Lieutenant General Michael Flynn, who had been appointed national security adviser, resigned in February 2017 primarily because he had conversations with officials from Russia before Trump became president, which, some believed, violated a law. However, since

Michael Flynn was part of the president's team and since it was only a matter of time before Trump was in the White House, such conversations by members of an elected president's team are not unusual or illegal. Of course, this was made public after Flynn had endured a lengthy investigation by agents of the Federal Bureau of Investigation (FBI)—an investigation that was highly questionable primarily because of the document on which the investigation was initiated.[9] President Trump soon appointed Lieutenant General H. R. McMaster as national security adviser.

In March 2017, President Trump began to fulfill the promises he had made on the campaign trail when he signed an executive order instructing the Environmental Protection Agency (EPA) that the administration would withdraw from the Paris Climate Accord (former President Obama had agreed to it).[10] In short, Trump believed the agreement penalized the United States by stifling the country's producers of energy. He announced the news to the American people a few months later.

When the Syrian government used chemical weapons to attack its own people in April 2017, the United States military fired missiles at an air base in Syria. Later the same month the military of the United States, Great Britain, and France fired missiles at Syria's facilities that produced chemical weapons.

In May 2017, President Trump fired James Comey, the director of the FBI, primarily because Comey had failed to do the job to his satisfaction. Comey and his subordinates had been investigating Michael Flynn and others who had worked on Trump's presidential campaign or transition team and whether any had connections to members of the Russian government.

The same month Deputy Attorney General Rod Rosenstein of the United States Department of Justice appointed Robert Mueller, the former director of the FBI, to oversee the Justice Department's investigation into the interference of the 2016 presidential election by the Russians.

Attorney General of the United States, Jeff Sessions, recused himself from the United States Department of Justice investigation into

Russian interference in the 2016 presidential election. (Jeff Sessions was fired in late 2018 and replaced by William Barr.) The FBI and the CIA claimed that certain groups in Russia had hacked into the computers of the Democratic National Committee and had released information to the public. Of course, members of the American press concluded that these groups had been working with one or more people associated with Trump's presidential campaign. When their stories appeared in the American press, President Trump claimed the stories were nothing more than "fake news."[11]

Later, the Trump administration developed a new travel ban for other countries. This ban, too, was soon blocked by one or more federal judges. Eventually, in June 2018, the United States Supreme Court sided with the administration.

In July 2017, Congress passed legislation that provided additional sanctions against Russia. Mostly Democratic members believed Russia had interfered in the 2016 presidential election. In response to the action by Congress, President Vladimir Putin of Russia ordered that the United States Embassy in Russia cut its staff by more than 700 people.

The same month federal agents raided Paul Manafort's home. Manafort was the former manager of Trump's presidential campaign. Later, Manafort was found guilty of money laundering, tax fraud, and conspiring against the country for his work with Ukrainian political interests, among other charges. Manafort was sentenced to prison.

In August 2017, in Charlottesville, Virginia, a confrontation erupted when large groups protested the removal of a statue of Confederate General Robert E. Lee. Purportedly, a man from Ohio who had marched with a so-called white supremacist group drove his car into a crowd of antiracist demonstrators. As a result, a woman was killed and almost 20 were injured. Although President Trump initially blamed all sides for the incident, which caused certain members, mostly Democrats, of Congress and the American press to condemn his remarks, he later denounced all hate groups. However, certain members, primarily Democrats, of Congress and the American press never forgot his initial remarks.

The same month Hurricane Harvey caused flooding in Texas. In September 2017, Hurricane Irma and Hurricane Maria caused major damage in Puerto Rico. In fact, the island's electrical and water infrastructures were impacted, which effected medical facilities. Thousands of people died. President Trump visited the island several weeks later.

Trump visited with leaders of numerous countries at a North Atlantic Treaty Organization (NATO) meeting in Europe. Believing the United States had been taken advantage of by other countries, Trump expressed that other member nations needed to increase their annual support of the organization, especially its military operations. Trump also attended the G-7 (Group of Seven) meeting in Europe in 2017. The latter met again in Canada the following year.

In December 2017, President Trump recognized Jerusalem as the capital of Israel. Consequently, he announced that the United States would move its embassy to the city. The same month he signed into law the Tax Cuts and Jobs Act, which he had asked Congress to pass. The act cut tax rates for corporations and individuals. It also eliminated the Individual Mandate that penalized individuals who did not purchase health insurance. The Individual Mandate was part of the Patient Protection and Affordable Care Act (Obamacare). When the act went into effect at the federal level, however, congresses of certain states passed legislation that included individual mandates pertaining to health insurance. As a result, individuals residing in these states had to have health insurance or pay a penalty.

In February 2018, the Mueller probe indicted several Russian individuals and several Russian organizations for interfering in the political and electoral processes of the United States during the 2016 presidential election.

In April 2018, the Trump administration developed a "zero-tolerance" immigration policy. In essence, all adults who entered the United States illegally would be criminally prosecuted. Children would be placed in shelters managed by the Office of Refugee Resettlement (ORR), a division of the Department of Health and Human Services (HHS), or in private shelters. In June, primarily because of criticism,

President Trump ended the separation of children from their parents. Nonetheless, Immigration and Customs Enforcement (ICE) agents were given the green light to arrest undocumented immigrants. As a result, mayors and governors declared their cities and states sanctuaries for illegal immigrants. In short, they refused to cooperate with ICE agents.

In May 2018, President Trump announced that the United States would withdraw from the Iranian nuclear deal that had been signed by President Obama and leaders of other countries. The deal had become controversial as a result of the former president giving millions of dollars to the Iranian government.

In June 2018, President Trump met with Kim Jong Un, the leader of North Korea, in Singapore. They discussed nuclear weapons in North Korea, among other topics. The two met again at the Demilitarized Zone between North and South Korea in 2019. They discussed nuclear weapons again, but no agreement was reached.

In July 2018, the Mueller probe indicted several Russian military officers for conspiring to interfere in the 2016 presidential election. According to the indictments, these officers were responsible for stealing thousands of e-mails from the Democratic Party and the Clinton campaign.

The same month President Trump met with President Putin of Russia in Finland. According to the president, he asked Putin if Russia had interfered in the presidential election of 2016. Putin claimed the Russian government had not. Trump believed Putin, which caused certain members of Congress as well as the American press to criticize him.

The same month the tariff war with China started, when President Trump placed 25 percent tariffs on more than 1,000 products made in that country. (China is a Communist country. Many serving in Congress seem to not know or have forgotten this fact.) Later, Trump placed more tariffs on products made in China.

In November 2018, President Trump, along with President Enrique Nieto of Mexico and Prime Minister Justin Trudeau of Canada, signed the United States-Mexico-Canada Agreement (USMCA), a new trade agreement that would eventually replace the North American Free

Trade Agreement (NAFTA). The agreement was approved by the United States Senate in 2020.

The same month Michael Cohen, a lawyer for Trump, pleaded guilty to lying to Congress about the details of a Trump real estate deal in Russia during the presidential campaign in 2016. Cohen was sentenced to prison as well.

President Trump was proud of the First Step Act, which reformed the criminal justice system by reducing mandatory minimum sentences for felonies related to drugs and which became law in December 2018. The act also expanded the early-release program and provided rehabilitation and job-training opportunities to inmates, among other provisions.

In February 2019, the Senate finally passed a spending bill that contained more than one billion dollars for the wall between Mexico and the United States. However, the bill allocated considerably less than what President Trump had requested.[12]

When Mueller submitted his report to Attorney General William Barr in March 2019, the Justice Department released a redacted version in April. Mueller could not prove that President Trump had been involved in any collusion with the Russians during the presidential election of 2016. In essence, Trump had not been found to have committed obstruction.

Primarily because the Mueller report failed to provide ammunition that could be used to impeach President Trump, the Democrats looked elsewhere. In 2019 they believed President Trump had urged President Volodymyr Zelensky of Ukraine to investigate former Vice President Joe Biden and his son Hunter Biden. Joe Biden eventually became the leading Democratic candidate for president.

Later the same year the Democrats in the House of Representatives approved two articles of impeachment: abuse of power and obstruction of Congress. When the articles went to the United States Senate, the majority believed the president was not guilty of having committed either article.[13]

In October 2019, Trump and the leader of Japan signed a trade deal at the White House. The same month the United States military killed Abu Bakr al-Baghdadi, the leader of ISIS, in Syria.

President Trump's economic policies turned the economy of the United States around. In fact, the economy reached historic highs in two to three years. In 2019, for instance, the unemployment rate was 3.7 percent, the lowest it had been since the 1960s. In addition, families were saving several thousand dollars on their federal income taxes. At the time, the president's poll number was high, especially when it was compared to the poll numbers of the previous two presidents or to members in Congress.

In January 2020, the United States military killed one of Iran's top generals, Qassem Soleimani, in Baghdad, Iraq. Soleimani had been responsible for attacks on the United States military installations in the Middle East, according to the Trump administration. A few days later Iran's military launched missiles at the United States military in Iraq, but no soldiers were killed.

The same month Trump and the leaders of China signed a trade agreement. This agreement, which took months, was merely the first President Trump hoped to sign between the two powers. Unfortunately, his attention had to focus on a lethal coronavirus that had originated in Wuhan, China. After Covid-19 arrived in the United States, the president announced that most businesses had to close for a brief period. At the time, the unemployment rate had decreased to 3.5 percent. Trump signed the Coronavirus Aid, Relief, and Economic Security Act (CARES), a major economic stimulus bill of two trillion dollars. Another smaller relief act was passed and signed a few days later. Trump informed the American people that several companies were working on vaccines for the virus. In fact, he stated that one or more vaccines would be available before the end of the year primarily because of his administration's so-called WARP SPEED policy. Although many health officials and members of the American press doubted whether vaccines could be developed, approved, and made available by the end of the year, Trump was correct. At least two vaccines were developed, approved, and made available. President Trump put Vice President Mike Pence in charge of the coronavirus task force.

Unfortunately, the closure caused millions of Americans to lose their jobs. In April 2020, the unemployment rate was more than 14 percent. As if the coronavirus was not grave enough, in May 2020, George Floyd, an African-American, died while in police custody in Minneapolis, Minnesota. His death caused demonstrations in cities across the country. Many of these demonstrations erupted into looting, burning, and physical violence. As a result, businesses were looted and burned, and several people were killed.

The coronavirus infected millions of Americans. Several hundred thousand died from it before any vaccines were developed, approved, and made available to the public. To say the least, President Trump and his administration saw the strong economy tumble. As a result of the coronavirus, in July 2020, the president announced that the United States was withdrawing from the World Health Organization, primarily because the organization had done little for the country.[14] Yet, the United States had given millions of dollars to it over the years.

In September 2020, at the White House, the United States helped broker a deal to normalize relations between Israel, the United Arab Emirates, and Bahrain. Later, the administration and Israel invited other countries. The same month Trump nominated Amy Coney Barrett as a justice of the United States Supreme Court. Although his nominee received criticism from certain Democratic members of Congress, she was confirmed by the United States Senate a month later.

In November 2020, the coronavirus was a monster. More Americans became infected and died. Still, the economy improved. Not only did the stock market bounce back, but the unemployment rate decreased to under 7 percent, as more town, city, and state governments allowed more and more businesses to open. Of course, most people wore masks and kept their distance from others whenever in public in an effort to limit the spread of the virus. They also washed their hands more often.

The same month Trump lost the presidential election primarily because several states allowed numerous mail-in ballots that were questionable or suspect, according to the administration. In fact, numerous states mailed out several ballots to each house, regardless of whether anyone at the house had requested any whatsoever. This should have caused alarm, not to mention outrage, in voters. They should have complained to those responsible and demanded another election that did not include mail-in ballots.

Although President Trump's number of votes set a record for any sitting president, many Americans believed Joe Biden's more than 81 million votes was utterly ridiculous. As a result, millions of Republicans and Independents did not believe that Joe Biden had actually won the election. Consequently, these people did not accept him as the president of the United States.

President Trump did not believe Biden had won, either. In fact, on Trump's behalf, several lawyers attempted to bring evidence before judges, but each refused to listen. Of course, this action by the judges only caused more suspicion about the election in the American people.

In January 2021, a rally was held in Washington, D.C., and President Trump spoke to the thousands of Americans who had gathered. Unfortunately, many people who may or may not have attended the rally stormed the capitol. As a result, several individuals died. Many Democratic members of Congress claimed the president had been responsible for inciting the people. Consequently, they hastily reacted by calling for the vice president to relieve the president (see the Twenty-fifth Amendment). Since Vice President Pence apparently understood the Twenty-fifth Amendment, he did not take any action against the president. The Democrats in the House of Representatives voted to impeach the president a second time. However, President Trump just had a few days left in office. The United States Senate did not have time to consider the articles of impeachment before Trump left office. As if members of the United States Senate had never read the *Constitution of the United States*, several, especially Democrats, exhibited their ignorance by claiming the senate could hold an impeachment trial after the president left office. (The founders, including Madison, would find such action unconstitutional.) Nonetheless, an impeachment trial was held in February 2021, but it was not overseen by the Chief Justice of the

Supreme Court. Although several Republican senators voted with the Democrats, there were not enough votes to find the president guilty.

In addition to the accomplishments mentioned above, Trump succeeded in getting numerous federal judges confirmed by the United States Senate. He also formally established the Space Force, which became the sixth branch of the United States Armed Forces, before he left office in 2020.

* * *

The new century started with Y2K, or the fear of computers failing. Apparently professional technicians solved the potential problems because few, if any, computers or servers failed.

In 2000 Republican George W. Bush, the oldest son of President George H. W. Bush, became president after the United States Supreme Court basically stopped the recount of votes in Florida. Later, after an investigation, the American press declared George W. Bush had received more votes than Democrat Al Gore in Florida.

The same year America Online announced that it was purchasing Time Warner Communications primarily because of Time Warner's assets and sales. The deal actually closed a year later.

The same year members of Al-Qaeda attacked the *USS Cole*, a guided missile destroyer, in Yemen, killing almost 20 sailors and wounding almost 40.

In September 2001, the United States experienced what its enemies were capable of doing, when four groups of terrorists skyjacked four commercial airplanes. Two of the planes crashed into the twin towers of the World Trade Center in New York City; one crashed into the Pentagon building in Washington, D.C.; and one crashed in a field in Pennsylvania. About 3,000 people were killed, and Osama Bin Laden and his Al-Qaeda terrorist organization were responsible for the diabolical acts, which initiated President Bush's war on terror.

After the September 2001 attack, letters containing Anthrax were mailed to several news media as well as to several United States Senators. As a result, at least five people were killed and almost 20 were wounded. The person responsible was never apprehended.

To say the least, President George W. Bush and his administration had their hands full. Indeed, the war on terror and the letters containing Anthrax filled time on 24-hour news stations and networks, not to mention space in newspapers and magazines. Many Americans were concerned, but because of the healthy economy they had jobs to do.

The United Nations Security Council issued a resolution that demanded Osama Bin Laden and others of Al-Qaeda be turned over to the United States. When the Taliban of Afghanistan refused, the military of the United States and other countries invaded the country and forced the Taliban out of it. However, it took the United States military 10 years to locate and kill Bin Laden.

In 2002 the Enron Corporation declared bankruptcy. Originally, the company had been a producer of energy; however, when it declared bankruptcy, it had become a trader of energy. The company had reported sales that were fraudulent and had hidden actual losses. The top executives were charged with insider trading, among other crimes.

In 2003 space shuttle Columbia disintegrated. Seven astronauts were killed.

As if the war in Afghanistan was not grave enough, President George W. Bush got the green light from Congress in 2003 to go after Saddam Hussein in Iraq. This was the start of the Iraq War, which lasted years.

Later in 2003, the northeastern United States experienced a blackout that effected millions of households.

In 2004 the American press reported that Iraqi prisoners had been tortured by American military forces at the Abu Ghraib prison. Eventually, several officers and soldiers were charged and sentenced to various terms in military prisons.

A year later Hurricane Katrina devastated the Gulf Coast, including New Orleans. In fact, the city flooded after several levees broke. In total, more than one million people were displaced. The storm's economic impact was hundreds of billions of dollars.

In 2006 Elon Musk introduced the Tesla Roadster, a new electric car. Tesla Motors had been founded in 2004. As a result of more interest in electric cars, Tesla introduced other models over the years.

In 2007 Apple unveiled the iPhone, which eventually changed how many people communicated. Unfortunately, the same year a student at Virginia Polytechnic Institute killed more than 30 students and wounded almost 20 before he killed himself.

In 2008 Lehman Brothers, a large bank, declared bankruptcy. Although this was not the cause of the financial crisis at the time, it made President Bush's administration realize the crisis was growing worse. Banks and other lenders were packaging mortgages and then selling these packages to other banks and companies. Unfortunately, prices of houses, which had been high, decreased. As a result, homeowners found it difficult to refinance their houses and began to default on their mortgages. The value of packages of mortgages declined. Lehman's losses were significant, to say the least. Eventually, its stock value plummeted. Although the bank tried to interest other banks into purchasing it, it failed. Bankruptcy was the only option left.

In 2008 Senator Barack Obama became the president of the United States. Although he faced a major recession, in June 2009, General Motors, the largest manufacturer of cars and trucks in the United States, declared bankruptcy, which made the recession worse. However, President Obama and the federal government reacted by providing financial support.

In 2010 President Obama signed the Patient Protection and Affordable Care Act (Obamacare), which mandated that people had to have health insurance through their employers or through the federal government. The same year he declared the United States military officially had ended its role in Iraq.

In 2012 Hurricane Sandy struck New Jersey and New York, causing a large storm surge along the coast. Almost two hundred people were killed. Losses were estimated at more than $50 billion. As if this was not grave enough, a year later two bombs exploded during the Boston Marathon, killing three people and wounding more than 250. Two brothers born in Krygystan were responsible.

In 2015 a young white supremacist killed nine people primarily because they were African-Americans at the Emanuel African Methodist Episcopal Church in Charleston, South Carolina.

The same year the United States Supreme Court ruled that each state had to recognize Same-Sex Marriage.

In 2016 Donald Trump, a businessman who had never held a political office, became the president of the United States by defeating former Secretary of State Hillary Clinton.

A year later the American people learned that hackers had infiltrated the data servers at Equifax, a major credit concern that had information on almost 150 million Americans.

In 2018 President Trump met Chairman Kim Jong Un of North Korea at a summit in Singapore. He was the first American president to do so. The same year Robert Bowers entered the Tree of Life Synagogue in Pittsburgh, Pennsylvania, and killed 11 people and wounded six others, including several police officers.

In 2019 President Trump ended the longest federal government shutdown when he signed a three-week continuing resolution. Trump had refused to sign a resolution earlier because he had not received any funds for building the wall between the United States and Mexico.

The same year the House of Representatives approved two articles of impeachment against President Trump. Although the articles were passed to the United States Senate, the majority acquitted the president of both articles.

In 2020 the coronavirus (COVID-19) spread from Wuhan, China, to all over the world, including the United States. The president ordered all but essential businesses to close for a brief period. Although unemployment was at 3.5 percent at the time, millions of Americans lost their jobs and had to file for unemployment. As a result, unemployment reached 14.7 percent in April, the highest number since the Great Depression. By November unemployment had improved to under 7 percent, as more businesses were allowed to open. Unfortunately, millions of Americans became infected with the virus. Several hundred thousand Americans died before vaccines were developed, approved, and made available.

The same year Space-X Endeavor was launched from Cape Kennedy. Its destination was the International Space Station. The crew returned successfully several months later. This was the first manned space flight on a privately built and funded rocket and space shuttle.

During the first two decades of the new century many Americans escaped reality by abusing opioids. In fact, thousands died each year from overdoses. Thousands more committed suicide. Without question, many Americans suffered from psychological problems.

Although violent crime decreased between 2000 and 2020, hate crimes increased.

Americans had grown afraid of foreign hackers invading their computers, tablets, and smart phones. They were not aware that the National Security Agency was gathering information about them. On the other hand, Americans provided certain information to specific social media such as Facebook, which had been founded in 2004, or Twitter, which had been founded in 2006, primarily because they were interested in communicating with relatives and friends.

President Barack Obama was concerned about the environment and the climate, but leaders of other countries were not. For instance, the so-called G20 countries had set goals to reduce their emissions, but only half had met these goals by 2020. Not only that, the citizens of Brazil, one of the largest countries in South America, had seen more of their country's forests disappear because of progress. The citizens of China experienced air pollution because of more coal-based electrical plants being built. The citizens of India and Russia experienced the same problem.

By 2020 Congress had more than one Democratic member that was a socialist. In fact, by 2020 most Democrats serving in Congress had a higher opinion of socialism than they did of capitalism. The possible reason for this change is the numerous Democratic members who had been elected to Congress during the past 20 years. These members apparently had not studied economics. If they had, they certainly would not have been in favor of socialism. (The founders of this country would be surprised at the number of socialistic programs we have now. Most, if not all, of these programs were introduced by Democrats.)

A few years ago most members of Congress believed that nine justices serving on the United States Supreme Court were enough. They also believed the Electoral College was necessary. By 2020 many of these members believed the Supreme Court needed more justices. Many also believed the Electoral College should be abolished.

Since 2000 there have been several large retailers, including K-mart and Sears, among others, that have gone out of business, as more Americans have learned to shop online. During this time Amazon grew into a giant retailer, making its primary owner one of the wealthiest individuals in the world.

By 2020 the influence the United States had in the world was less than it had been in 2000, according to certain individuals in Washington, D.C. Whether this is true is debatable.

Notes:

1. Philosophically, the Bush administration was correct. The articles of the Geneva Conventions did not apply to terrorists who had been apprehended by the United States military. The articles of the Geneva Conventions were for prisoners of war—that is, military service men and women who were fighting for a recognized country that had declared war on another recognized country, not terrorists who were fighting for a so-called ideology to which no country subscribed.
2. The Bush administration basically claimed water boarding and similar techniques were not torture. In addition, since the prisoners were held in prisons outside the United States, the United States Uniform Code of Military Justice did not apply, especially if the prisons were not managed by any military branch of the United States. Furthermore, the articles of the Geneva Conventions did not apply to terrorists (see above).
3. Overall, criticism of President Barack Obama or his administration by members of the American press was rare during his eight years in office, which is not unusual for a Democratic president. Indeed, most members of the American press typically refrain from criticizing a Democratic president or Democratic administration primarily because many members of the press are liberal and/or are members of the Democratic Party. This is not the author's opinion. Rather, this is based on studies that have been conducted over several decades. For instance, see one or more studies by S. Robert Lichter and Stanley Rothman; or see S. Robert Lichter, Stanley Rothman, and Linda S. Lichter, *The Media Elite: America's New Powerbrokers*, which was published in 1990; or see David Weaver,

et al., *The American Journalist in the 21st Century*, which was published in 2014. Of course, there are similar studies by other authors, too.

4. The reader should remember, too, that millions of Americans had grown disillusioned with their federal government, especially after the 1990s, when many who had been elected to Congress had promised they would pass legislation limiting the number of terms people could serve in Congress. Yet, such legislation never passed. So, many Republicans reacted by not voting for one of the typical political candidates running in 2016. Instead, they selected Trump, a man who actually owned a large diverse company, which is rare when one examines the backgrounds of those who have served as president. In fact, it is rare for anyone serving in Congress to have owned a business, let alone a diverse company like Trump's.

Perhaps Americans who vote need to investigate the backgrounds of those who run for Congress and ask themselves what have these people actually accomplished. Furthermore, Americans need to learn if the person is for capitalism, socialism, or Communism. The latter two have not been *that* successful wherever either has been tried. In fact, the latter two conflict with the foundational philosophy of the United States. Furthermore, Americans need to read each political party's platform and ask themselves if they subscribe to the party's policies. After all, each elected individual invariably will follow the party's platform. (Basically, they have no choice.) When someone runs for reelection, American voters need to learn what the person accomplished during his/her term in Congress. If the person was not responsible for a piece of legislation that helped his/her constituents, then the person should not be reelected. ***It is this simple.*** Primarily because everyone aged 18 and over have the right to vote, is it little wonder that there are so many seemingly ignorant and/or self-centered individuals serving in Congress? Perhaps not everyone aged 18 should be allowed to vote. Perhaps only those who pay federal income taxes each year should be allowed to vote for members of Congress and the president. After all, these people are paying for most of the country's bills, so to speak. Besides, this would eliminate almost half of those allowed to vote now. This change would more than likely eliminate possible fraudulent problems, such as mail-in ballots, which, by the way, should be made illegal by every state. Indeed, each voter should be required to vote in person, especially in a presidential election. In addition, each voter should be required to show an identification card with a photograph as well as be required to sign a voting form. After all, voting in the United States should be taken seriously by each voter and each elected official. If state legislatures desire to change rules regarding voting in their states, they should do so months before the first candidate starts his/her campaign. Indeed, state legislatures should not change the rules after the first candidate has started his/her campaign.

5. People who typically work for the federal government are used to getting off every federal holiday and weekend. They also are used to getting lengthy vacations and higher salaries than those who work in the private sector. (For instance, the average salary in Washington, D.C., is about $110,000 per year (2020). This does not include bonuses or raises. This is more than the average salary of those who have a comparable position in the private sector.) People who serve in Congress are used to even easier working schedules and higher salaries. Indeed, these people work on average two to two-and-a-half days each week Congress is in session and earn $174,000 per year (2020). Leaders of the House of Representatives and the Senate earn considerably more. In short, these people are highly overpaid for what they accomplish, which is very little when compared to others who work for industries and businesses. As a matter of fact, after many years of so-called public service, numerous members of Congress can retire and earn considerably more than most of their constituents. Yet, many did not produce one major piece of legislation that helped their constituents while they served.

As of this writing, the average age of a United States Senator serving in the United States Senate is 64 (2021). The average age of a representative serving in the United States House of Representatives is 58 (2021). However, the Speaker of the House is 80 years old (2021). The Majority Leader of the United States Senate is 70 (2021). The President is 78 (2021). Should these elderly people be running the country?

6. The question is should a federal judge—not a United States Supreme Court justice, by the way—who is appointed and not elected by the people have more power than an elected president?

7. Of course, these suits were not filed based on actual evidence. They were filed based on possible violation.

8. In short, these senators asked idiotic questions that sounded like a staff member or someone from the Democratic Party had written them. Of course, since several of the senators had been lawyers before they had become members of the United States Senate, they may have written them. (Unfortunately, law schools do not provide a sound and broad education. Indeed, most of these schools require courses in law, nothing more, not even courses in the history of law

or ethics, which are generally offered as electives. Thus, most graduates of law schools do not know that many laws in the United States can be traced to the Old Testament. Whereas other so-called professional schools provide a more sound and much broader education. Consequently, law schools need to reexamine their curriculums. Furthermore, several so-called elite law schools do not give grades in the courses offered during a student's first year. After the first year, these schools do not give letter grades, but pass, or low pass, or something similar.) Anyway, the process was embarrassing to any intelligent American who watched it. (By the way, those elected to Congress or the presidency are not required to pass a test on the founding documents on which the country is based. In fact, those elected do not even have to read these documents before they take office.) (This author believes that anyone running for the presidency, the United States Senate, or the House of Representatives should be required to pass a test that contains questions about the founders and the *Declaration of Independence*, the *Constitution of the United States*, and the *Amendments to the Constitution*. In short, these offices are important and should be held by intelligent individuals who have been productive over the years, not held by political hacks who are controlled by various special interests, including foreign governments.)

9. Of course, Flynn should not have pleaded guilty to lying to any agent of the FBI about his actions, especially if one or more agents had coerced him into doing so.
10. Unfortunately, at the time the agreement was signed by President Obama, members of the American press apparently had not read it because they did not share the details of it with the American people. If they had, many Americans would have complained about it.
11. The American press, including the so-called news stations and networks, laid off thousands of reporters in the early 2000s. As a result, fewer employees were responsible for the content found in newspapers, radio stations, television stations, and television networks. Consequently, so-called "fake news" became a reality, especially on the so-called news stations and networks, not to mention social media. Prominent investigative reporters and journalism professors have investigated this subject. In fact, the so-called news stations and networks that discuss politics typically present stories filled with innuendo, opinion, and/or speculation. In short, these stories are not necessarily based on every fact. Instead, they are biased or slanted, depending on the station's or network's agenda, and heavily opinionated. For more information about "fake news," see Seymour

Hersh, *Reporter: A Memoir* (2018), Melissa Zimdars and Kembrew McLeod, eds., *Fake News: Understanding Media and Misinformation in the Digital Age* (2020), and/or Nolan Higdon, *The Anatomy of Fake News: A Critical News Literacy Education* (2020). Of course, there are numerous other books about the subject.

12. Thousands of people illegally entered the United States during President Trump's years in the White House. In 2019, however, the administration initiated a "remain in Mexico" policy, which caused the annual figures to decrease.
13. Of course, any intelligent American realized that the Democrats had developed the articles of impeachment primarily to embarrass the president before the presidential election. The second impeachment was unconstitutional for several reasons: senators did not follow the constitution; Donald Trump was no longer president; Chief Justice John Roberts was not present; and the so-called trial did not include witnesses. Of course, there was another problem: the president never told anyone to storm the Capitol of the United States.
14. In fact, the United States had given millions of dollars to this organization over the years and had received little in return.

References:

Baker, Peter. *Days of Fire: Bush and Cheney in the White House*. New York: Anchor, 2014.

Baker, Peter. *Obama: The Call of History*. New York: New York Times/Callaway, 2017.

Black, Conrad. *Donald J. Trump: A President Like No Other*. Washington, D.C.: Regnery Publishing, 2018.

Blair, Gwenda. *The Trumps: Three Generations That Built an Empire*. New York: Simon & Schuster, 2000.

Garrow, David. *Rising Star: The Making of Barack Obama*. New York: William Morrow, 2017.

Herbert, Jon, Trevor McCrisken, and Andrew Wroe. *The Ordinary Presidency of Donald J. Trump*. London: Palgrave Macmillan, 2019.

Kranish, Michael and Marc Fisher. *Trump Revealed: The Definitive Biography of the 45th President*. New York: Simon & Schuster, 2016.

Maraniss, David. *Barack Obama: The Story*. New York: Simon & Schuster, 2012.

Remnick, David. *The Bridge: The Life and Rise of Barack Obama*. New York: Knopf, 2010.

Smith, Jean Edward. *Bush*. New York: Simon & Schuster, 2016.

Appendix A

Presidents of the United States and the National Debt*

President	Dates	Starting Debt ($)	Ending Debt ($)
George Washington	1789-1797	71,060,508	82,064,479
John Adams	1797-1801	82,064,479	83,038,050
Thomas Jefferson	1801-1809	83,038,050	57,023,192
James Madison	1809-1817	54,023,192	123,491,965
James Monroe	1817-1825	123,491,965	83,788,432
John Q. Adams	1825-1829	83,788,432	58,421,413
Andrew Jackson	1829-1837	58,421,413	336,957
Martin Van Buren	1837-1841	336,957	5,250,875
Wm. H. Harrison	1841	5,250,875	5,250,875
John Tyler	1841-1845	5,250,875	15,925,303
James Polk	1845-1849	15,925,303	63,061,858
Zachary Taylor	1849-1850	63,061,858	63,452,773
Millard Fillmore	1850-1853	63,452,773	59,803,117
Franklin Pierce	1853-1857	59,803,117	28,699,831
James Buchanan	1857-1861	28,699,831	90,588,873
Abraham Lincoln	1861-1865	90,580,873	2,680,647,869
Andrew Johnson	1865-1869	2,680,647,869	2,588,452,213
Ulysses S. Grant	1869-1877	2,588,452,213	2,205,301,392
Rutherford B. Hayes	1877-1881	2,205,301,392	2,069,013,569
James Garfield	1881	2,069,013,569	2,069,013,569
Chester A. Arthur	1881-1885	2,069,013,569	1,863,964,873
Grover Cleveland	1885-1889	1,863,964,873	1,619,052,922
Benjamin Harrison	1889-1893	1,619,052,922	1,545,985,686

Grover Cleveland	1893-1897	1,545,985,686	1,817,672,665
Wm. McKinley	1897-1901	1,817,672,665	2,143,326,933
Theodore Roosevelt	1901-1909	2,143,326,933	2,639,546,241
Wm. H. Taft	1909-1913	2,639,546,241	2,916,204,913
Woodrow Wilson	1913-1921	2,916,204,913	23,977,450,552
Warren G. Harding	1921-1923	23,977,450,552	22,349,707,365
Calvin Coolidge	1923-1929	22,349,707,365	16,931,088,484
Herbert Hoover	1929-1933	16,931,088,484	22,538,672,560
F. D. Roosevelt	1933-1945	22,538,672,560	258,682,187,409
Harry S. Truman	1945-1953	258,682,187,409	266,071,061,638
Dwight Eisenhower	1953-1961	266,071,061,638	288,970,938,610
John F. Kenndy	1961-1963	288,970,938,610	305,859,632,996
Lyndon Johnson	1963-1969	305,859,632,996	353,720,253,841
Richard Nixon	1969-1974	353,720,253,841	475,059,815,731
Gerald Ford	1974-1977	475,059,815,731	698,840,000,000
Jimmy Carter	1977-1981	698,840,000,000	997,855,000,000
Ronald Reagan	1981-1989	997,855,000,000	2,857,430,960,187
George H. W. Bush	1989-1993	2,857,430,960,187	4,411,488,883,139
Wm. J. Clinton	1993-2001	4,411,488,883,139	5,807,463,412,200
George W. Bush	2001-2009	5,807,463,412,200	11,909,829,003,511
Barack Obama	2009-2017	11,909,829,003,511	20,244,900,016,053
Donald Trump	2017-2021	20,244,900,016,053	27,052,190,118,519

***The information in this table is from information at the following: (www.whitehouse.gov/omb/historical-tables).**

Appendix B

Unemployment Rates for Each President Since 1929*

Unemployment Rates		
President	**First Year of Office**	**Last Year of Office**
Herbert Hoover	1929—3.2%	1933—24.9%
F. D. Roosevelt	1933—24.9%	1945—1.9%[1]
Harry Truman	1945—1.9%	1953—2.9%
Dwight Eisenhower	1953—2.9%	1961—6.7%
John F. Kennedy	1961—6.7%	1963—5.7%
Lyndon Johnson	1963—5.7%	1969—3.5%[2]
Richard Nixon	1969—3.5%	1974—5.6%
Gerald Ford	1974—5.6%	1977—7.1%
Jimmy Carter	1977—7.1%	1981—7.6%
Ronald Reagan	1981—7.6%	1989—5.3%
George H. W. Bush	1989—5.3%	1993—6.9%
Wm. J. Clinton	1993—6.9%	2001—4.7%
George W. Bush	2001—4.7%	2009—9.3%
Barack Obama	2009—9.3%	2017—4.4%
Donald J. Trump	2017—4.4%	2021—6.7%[3]

*The information in this table is from information at the following: "Databases, Tables & Calculators by Subject," U.S. Bureau of Labor Statistics, (**www.data.bls.gov/timeseries/**).

1. This low unemployment figure is because of World War II. Many men and women served in either the military or worked in factories that manufactured various equipment and weapons for the war.

2. This low unemployment figure is because of the president's many social programs and the Vietnam War.

3. This figure is misleading. When Covid-19 struck the United States, which was almost a year before the president left office, the unemployment figure was under 3.5%. As businesses shut down across the country, the unemployment figure increased to almost 15%. Months before the president left office, more and more businesses across the country opened. As a result, the unemployment figure decreased to 6.7%.

The reader should note the following Appendices are based on the original documents. Consequently, usage in these documents may differ from usage today.

Appendix C

Articles of Confederation and Perpetual Union*

(***This document, which was approved in 1781, provided a loose federal government before the Constitution was drafted and put into effect in 1789.***)

To all to whom these Presents shall come, we the undersigned Delegates of the States affixed to our Names send greeting.

Whereas the Delegates of the United States of America in Congress assembled did on the fifteenth day of November in the Year of our Lord One Thousand Seven Hundred and Seventy Seven, and in the Second Year of the Independence of America agree to certain articles of Confederation and perpetual Union between the States of New Hampshire, Massachusetts-bay, Rhode Island and Providence Plantations, Connecticut, New York, New Jersey, Pennsylvania, Delaware, Maryland, Virginia, North Carolina, South Carolina and Georgia.

Article I. The Stile of this Confederacy shall be "**The United States of America**."

Article II. Each state retains its sovereignty, freedom, and independence, and every power, jurisdiction, and right, which is not by this Confederation expressly delegated to the United States, in Congress assembled.

Article III. The said States hereby severally enter into a firm league of friendship with each other, for their common defence, the security of their liberties, and their mutual and general welfare, binding themselves to assist each other, against all force offered to, or attacks made upon them, or any of them, on account of religion, sovereignty, trade, or any other pretense whatever.

Article IV. The better to secure and perpetuate mutual friendship and intercourse among the people of the different States in this Union, the free inhabitants of each of these States, paupers, vagabonds, and fugitives from justice excepted, shall be entitled to all privileges and immunities of free citizens in the several States; and the people of each State shall free ingress and regress to and from any other State, and shall enjoy therein all the privileges of trade and commerce, subject to the same duties, impositions, and restrictions as the inhabitants thereof respectively, provided that such restrictions shall not extend so far as to prevent the removal of property imported into any State, to any other State, of which the owner is an inhabitant; provided also that no imposition, duties or restriction shall be laid by any State, on the property of the United States, or either of them.

If any person guilty of, or charged with, treason, felony, or other high misdemeanor in any State, shall flee from justice, and be found in any of the United States, he shall, upon demand of the Governor or executive power of the State from which he fled, be delivered up and removed to the State having jurisdiction of his offense.

Full faith and credit shall be given in each of these States to the records, acts, and judicial proceedings of the courts and magistrates of every other State.

Article V. For the most convenient management of the general interests of the United States, delegates shall be annually appointed in such manner as the legislatures of each State shall direct, to meet in Congress on the first Monday in November, in every year, with a power reserved to each State to recall its delegates, or any of them, at any time within the year, and to send others in their stead for the remainder of the year.

No State shall be represented in Congress by less than two, nor more than seven members; and no person shall be capable of being a delegate for more than three years in any term of six years; nor shall any person, being a delegate, be capable of holding any office under the United States, for which he, or another for his benefit, receives any salary, fees or emolument of any kind.

Each State shall maintain its own delegates in a meeting of the States, and while they act as members of the committee of the States.

In determining questions in the United States in Congress assembled, each State shall have one vote.

Freedom of speech and debate in Congress shall not be impeached or questioned in any court or place out of Congress, and the members of Congress shall be protected in their persons from arrests or imprisonments, during the time of their going to and from, and attendence on Congress, except for treason, felony, or breach of the peace.

Article VI. No State, without the consent of the United States in Congress assembled, shall send any embassy to, or receive any embassy from, or enter into any conference, agreement, alliance or treaty with any King, Prince or State; nor shall any person holding any office of profit or trust under the United States, or any of them, accept any present, emolument, office or title of any kind whatever from any King, Prince or foreign State; nor shall the United States in Congress assembled, or any of them, grant any title of nobility.

No two or more States shall enter into any treaty, confederation or alliance whatever between them, without the consent of the United States in Congress assembled, specifying accurately the purposes for which the same is to be entered into, and how long it shall continue.

No State shall lay any imposts or duties, which may interfere with any stipulations in treaties, entered into by the United States in Congress assembled, with any King, Prince or State, in pursuance of any treaties already proposed by Congress, to the courts of France and Spain.

No vessel of war shall be kept up in time of peace by any State, except such number only, as shall be deemed necessary by the United States in Congress assembled, for the defense of such State, or its trade; nor shall any body of forces be kept up by any State in time of peace, except such number only, as in the judgement of the United States in Congress assembled, shall be deemed requisite to garrison the forts necessary for the defense of such State; but every State shall always keep up a well-regulated and disciplined militia, sufficiently armed and accoutered, and shall provide and constantly have ready for use, in public stores, a due number of filed pieces and tents, and a proper quantity of arms, ammunition and camp equipage.

No State shall engage in any war without the consent of the United States in Congress assembled, unless such State be actually invaded by enemies, or shall have received certain advice of a resolution being formed by some nation of Indians to invade such State, and the danger is so imminent as not to admit of a delay till the United States in Congress assembled can be consulted; nor shall any State grant commissions to any ships or vessels of war, nor letters of marque or reprisal, except it be after a declaration of war by the United States in Congress assembled, and then only against the Kingdom or State and the subjects thereof, against which war has been so declared, and under such regulations as shall be established by the United States in Congress assembled, unless such State be infested by pirates, in which case vessels of war may be fitted out for that occasion, and kept so long as the danger shall continue, or until the United States in Congress assembled shall determine otherwise.

Article VII. When land forces are raised by any State for the common defense, all officers of or under the rank of colonel, shall be appointed by the legislature of each State respectively, by whom such forces shall be raised, or in such manner as such State shall direct, and all vacancies shall be filled up by the State which first made the appointment.

Article VIII. All charges of war, and all other expenses that shall be incurred for the common defense or general welfare, and allowed by the United States in Congress assembled, shall be defrayed out of a common treasury, which shall be supplied by the several States in proportion to the value of all land within each State, granted or surveyed for any person, as such land and the buildings and improvements thereon shall be estimated according to such mode as the United States in Congress assembled, shall from time to time direct and appoint.

The taxes for paying that proportion shall be laid and levied by the authority and direction of the legislatures of the several States within the time agreed upon by the United States in Congress assembled.

Article IX. The United States in Congress assembled, shall have the sole and exclusive right and power of determining on peace and war, except in the cases mentioned in the sixth article -- of sending and receiving ambassadors -- entering into treaties and alliances, provided that no treaty of commerce shall be made whereby the legislative power of the respective States shall be restrained from imposing such imposts and duties on foreigners, as their own people are subjected to, or from prohibiting the exportation or importation of any species of goods or commodities whatsoever -- of establishing rules for deciding in all cases, what captures on land or water shall be legal, and in what manner prizes taken by land or naval forces in the service of the United States shall be divided or appropriated -- of granting letters of marque and reprisal in times of peace -- appointing courts for the trial of piracies and felonies commited on the high seas and establishing courts for receiving and determining finally appeals in all cases of captures, provided that no member of Congress shall be appointed a judge of any of the said courts.

The United States in Congress assembled shall also be the last resort on appeal in all disputes and differences now subsisting or that hereafter may arise between two or more States concerning boundary, jurisdiction or any other causes whatever; which authority shall always be exercised in the manner following. Whenever the legislative or executive authority or lawful agent of any State in controversy with another shall present a petition to Congress stating the matter in question and praying for a hearing, notice thereof shall be given by order of Congress to the legislative or executive authority of the other State in controversy, and a day assigned for the appearance of the parties by their lawful agents, who shall then be directed to appoint by joint consent, commissioners or judges to constitute a court for hearing and determining the matter in question: but if they cannot agree, Congress shall name three persons out of each of the United States, and from the list of such persons each party shall alternately strike out one, the petitioners beginning, until the number shall be reduced to thirteen; and from that number not less than seven, nor more than nine names as Congress shall direct, shall in the presence of Congress be drawn out by lot, and the persons whose names shall be so drawn or any five of them, shall be commissioners or judges, to hear and finally determine the controversy, so always as a major part of the judges who shall hear the cause shall agree in the determination: and if either party shall neglect to attend at the day appointed, without showing reasons, which Congress shall judge sufficient, or being present shall refuse to strike, the Congress shall proceed to nominate three persons out of each State, and the secretary of Congress shall strike in behalf of such party absent or refusing; and the judgement and sentence of the court to be appointed, in the manner before prescribed, shall be final and conclusive; and if any of the parties shall refuse to submit to the authority of such court, or to appear or defend their claim or cause, the court shall nevertheless proceed to pronounce sentence, or judgement, which shall in like manner be final and decisive, the judgement or sentence and other proceedings being in either case transmitted to Congress, and lodged among the acts of Congress for the security of the parties concerned: provided that every commissioner, before he sits in judgement, shall take an oath to be administered by one of the judges of the supreme or superior court of the State, where the cause shall be tried, 'well and truly to hear and determine the matter in question, according to the best of his judgement, without favor, affection or hope of reward:' provided also, that no State shall be deprived of territory for the benefit of the United States.

All controversies concerning the private right of soil claimed under different grants of two or more States, whose jurisdictions as they may respect such lands, and the States which passed such grants are adjusted, the said grants or either of them being at the same time claimed to have originated antecedent to such settlement of jurisdiction, shall on the petition of either party to the Congress of the United States, be finally determined as near as may be in the same manner as is before presecribed for deciding disputes respecting territorial jurisdiction between different States.

The United States in Congress assembled shall also have the sole and exclusive right and power of regulating the alloy and value of coin struck by their own authority, or by that of the respective States -- fixing the standards of weights and measures throughout the United States -- regulating the trade and managing all affairs with the Indians, not members of any of the States, provided that the legislative right of any State within its own limits be not infringed or violated -- establishing or regulating post offices from one State to another, throughout all the United States, and exacting such postage on the papers passing through the same as may be requisite to defray the expenses of the said office -- appointing all officers of the land forces, in the service of the United States, excepting regimental officers – appointing all the officers of the naval forces, and commissioning all officers whatever in the service of the United States -- making rules for the government and regulation of the said land and naval forces, and directing their operations.

The United States in Congress assembled shall have authority to appoint a committee, to sit in the recess of Congress, to be denominated 'A Committee of the States,' and to consist of one delegate from each State; and to appoint such other committees and civil officers as may be necessary for managing the general affairs of the United States under their direction -- to appoint one of their members to preside, provided that no person be allowed to serve in the office of president more than one year in any term of three years; to ascertain the necessary sums of money to be raised for the service of the United States, and to appropriate and apply the same for defraying the public expenses -- to borrow money, or emit bills on the credit of the United States, transmitting every half-year to the respective States an account of the sums of money so borrowed or emitted -- to build and equip a navy -- to agree upon the number of land forces, and to make requisitions from each State for its quota, in proportion to the number of white inhabitants in such State; which requisition shall be binding, and thereupon the legislature of each State shall appoint the regimental officers, raise the men and cloath, arm and equip them in a solid-like manner, at the expense of the United States; and the officers and men so cloathed, armed and equipped shall march to the place appointed, and within the time agreed on by the United States in Congress assembled. But if the United States in Congress assembled shall, on consideration of circumstances judge proper that any State should not raise men, or should raise a smaller number of men than the quota thereof, such extra number shall be raised, officered, cloathed, armed and equipped in the same manner as the quota of each State, unless the legislature of such State shall judge that such extra number cannot be safely spread out in the same, in which case they shall raise, officer, cloath, arm and equip as many of such extra number as they judge can be safely spared. And the officers and men so cloathed, armed, and equipped, shall march to the place appointed, and within the time agreed on by the United States in Congress assembled.

The United States in Congress assembled shall never engage in a war, nor grant letters of marque or reprisal in time of peace, nor enter into any treaties or alliances, nor coin money, nor regulate the value thereof, nor ascertain the sums and expenses necessary for the defense and welfare of the United States, or any of them, nor emit bills, nor borrow money on the credit of the United States, nor appropriate money, nor agree upon the number of vessels of war, to be built or purchased, or the number of land or sea forces to be raised, nor appoint a commander in chief of the army or navy, unless nine States assent to the same: nor shall a question on any other point, except for adjourning from day to day be determined, unless by the votes of the majority of the United States in Congress assembled.

The Congress of the United States shall have power to adjourn to any time within the year, and to any place within the United States, so that no period of adjournment be for a longer duration than the space of six months, and shall publish the journal of their proceedings monthly, except such parts thereof relating to treaties, alliances or military operations, as in their judgement require secrecy; and the yeas and nays of the delegates of each State on any question shall be entered on the journal, when it is desired by any delegates of a State, or any of them, at his or their request shall be furnished with a transcript of the said journal, except such parts as are above excepted, to lay before the legislatures of the several States.

Article X. The Committee of the States, or any nine of them, shall be authorized to execute, in the recess of Congress, such of the powers of Congress as the United States in Congress assembled, by the consent of the nine States, shall from time to time think expedient to vest them with; provided that no power be delegated to the said Committee, for the exercise of which, by the Articles of Confederation, the voice of nine States in the Congress of the United States assembled be requisite.

Article XI. Canada acceding to this confederation, and adjoining in the measures of the United States, shall be admitted into, and entitled to all the advantages of this Union; but no other colony shall be admitted into the same, unless such admission be agreed to by nine States.

Article XII. All bills of credit emitted, monies borrowed, and debts contracted by, or under the authority of Congress, before the assembling of the United States, in pursuance of the present confederation, shall be deemed and considered as a charge against the United States, for payment and satisfaction whereof the said United States, and the public faith are hereby solemnly pleged.

Article XIII. Every State shall abide by the determination of the United States in Congress assembled, on all questions which by this confederation are submitted to them. And the Articles of this Confederation shall be inviolably observed by every State, and the Union shall be perpetual; nor shall any alteration at any time hereafter be made in any of them; unless such alteration be agreed to in a Congress of the United States, and be afterwards confirmed by the legislatures of every State.

And Whereas it hath pleased the Great Governor of the World to incline the hearts of the legislatures we respectively represent in Congress, to approve of, and to authorize us to ratify the said Articles of Confederation and perpetual Union. Know Ye that we the undersigned delegates, by virtue of the power and authority to us given for that purpose, do by these presents, in the name and in behalf of our respective constituents, fully and entirely ratify and confirm each and every of the said Articles of Confederation and perpetual Union, and all and singular the matters and things therein contained: And we do further solemnly plight and engage the faith of our respective constituents, that they shall abide by the determinations of the United States in Congress assembled, on all questions, which by the said Confederation are submitted to them. And that the Articles thereof shall be inviolably observed by the States we respectively represent, and that the Union shall be perpetual.

In Witness whereof we have hereunto set our hands in Congress. Done at Philadelphia in the State of Pennsylvania the ninth day of July in the Year of our Lord One Thousand Seven Hundred and Seventy-Eight, and in the Third Year of the independence of America.

Agreed to by Congress 15 November 1777 In force after ratification by Maryland, 1 March 1781

Virginia
George Wythe
Richard Henry Lee
Thomas Jefferson
Benjamin Harrison
Thomas Nelson, Jr.
Francis Lightfoot Lee
Carter Braxton

Pennsylvania
Robert Morris
Benjamin Rush
Benjamin Franklin
John Morton
George Clymer
James Smith
George Taylor
James Wilson
George Ross

New York
William Floyd
Philip Livingston
Francis Lewis
Lewis Morris

New Jersey
Richard Stockton
John Witherspoon
Francis Hopkinson
John Hart

Abraham Clark

New Hampshire
Josiah Bartlett
William Whipple

Massachusetts
John Hancock
Samuel Adams
John Adams
Robert Treat Paine
Elbridge Gerry

Rhode Island
Stephen Hopkins
William Ellery

Connecticut
Roger Sherman
Samuel Huntington
William Williams
Oliver Wolcott

New Hampshire
Matthew Thornton

Appendix D

Declaration of Independence

(This document, which was written primarily by Thomas Jefferson and provided numerous reasons for the 13 colonies to be independent from Great Britain, was adopted by the Continental Congress July 4, 1776. The Continental Congress governed under the Articles of Confederation and Perpetual Union during the Revolutionary War.)

IN CONGRESS, July 4, 1776

The unanimous Declaration of the thirteen united states of America,

When in the Course of human events, it becomes necessary for one people to dissolve the political bands which have connected them with another, and to assume among the powers of the earth, the separate and equal station to which the Laws of Nature and of Nature's God entitle them, a decent respect to the opinions of mankind requires that they should declare the causes which impel them to the separation.

We hold these truths to be self-evident, that all men are created equal, that they are endowed by their Creator with certain unalienable Rights, that among these are Life, Liberty and the pursuit of Happiness.--That to secure these rights, Governments are instituted among Men, deriving their just powers from the consent of the governed, --That whenever any Form of Government becomes destructive of these ends, it is the Right of the People to alter or to abolish it, and to institute new Government, laying its foundation on such principles and organizing its powers in such form, as to them shall seem most likely to effect their Safety and Happiness. Prudence, indeed, will dictate that Governments long established should not be changed for light and transient causes; and accordingly all experience hath shewn, that mankind are more disposed to suffer, while evils are sufferable, than to right themselves by abolishing the forms to which they are accustomed. But when a long train of abuses and usurpations, pursuing invariably the same Object evinces a design to reduce them under absolute Despotism, it is their right, it is their duty, to throw off such Government, and to provide new Guards for their future security.--Such has been the patient sufferance of these Colonies; and such is now the necessity which constrains them to alter their former Systems of Government. The history of the present King of Great Britain is a history of repeated injuries and usurpations, all having in direct object the establishment of an absolute Tyranny over these States. To prove this, let Facts be submitted to a candid world.

He has refused his Assent to Laws, the most wholesome and necessary for the public good.

He has forbidden his Governors to pass Laws of immediate and pressing importance, unless suspended in their operation till his Assent should be obtained; and when so suspended, he has utterly neglected to attend to them.

He has refused to pass other Laws for the accommodation of large districts of people, unless those people would relinquish the right of Representation in the Legislature, a right inestimable to them and formidable to tyrants only.

He has called together legislative bodies at places unusual, uncomfortable, and distant from the depository of their public Records, for the sole purpose of fatiguing them into compliance with his measures.

He has dissolved Representative Houses repeatedly, for opposing with manly firmness his invasions on the rights of the people.

He has refused for a long time, after such dissolutions, to cause others to be elected; whereby the Legislative powers, incapable of Annihilation, have returned to the People at large for their exercise; the State remaining in the mean time exposed to all the dangers of invasion from without, and convulsions within.

He has endeavoured to prevent the population of these States; for that purpose obstructing the Laws for Naturalization of Foreigners; refusing to pass others to encourage their migrations hither, and raising the conditions of new Appropriations of Lands.

He has obstructed the Administration of Justice, by refusing his Assent to Laws for establishing Judiciary powers.

He has made Judges dependent on his Will alone, for the tenure of their offices, and the amount and payment of their salaries.

He has erected a multitude of New Offices, and sent hither swarms of Officers to harrass our people, and eat out their substance.

He has kept among us, in times of peace, Standing Armies without the Consent of our legislatures.

He has affected to render the Military independent of and superior to the Civil power.

He has combined with others to subject us to a jurisdiction foreign to our constitution, and unacknowledged by our laws; giving his Assent to their Acts of pretended Legislation:

For Quartering large bodies of armed troops among us:

For protecting them, by a mock Trial, from punishment for any Murders which they should commit on the Inhabitants of these States:

For cutting off our Trade with all parts of the world:

For imposing Taxes on us without our Consent:

For depriving us in many cases, of the benefits of Trial by Jury:

For transporting us beyond Seas to be tried for pretended offences:

For abolishing the free System of English Laws in a neighbouring Province, establishing therein an Arbitrary government, and enlarging its Boundaries so as to render it at once an example and fit instrument for introducing the same absolute rule into these Colonies:

For taking away our Charters, abolishing our most valuable Laws, and altering fundamentally the Forms of our Governments:

For suspending our own Legislatures, and declaring themselves invested with power to legislate for us in all cases whatsoever.

He has abdicated Government here, by declaring us out of his Protection and waging War against us.

He has plundered our seas, ravaged our Coasts, burnt our towns, and destroyed the lives of our people.

He is at this time transporting large Armies of foreign Mercenaries to compleat the works of death, desolation and tyranny, already begun with circumstances of Cruelty & perfidy scarcely paralleled in the most barbarous ages, and totally unworthy the Head of a civilized nation.

He has constrained our fellow Citizens taken Captive on the high Seas to bear Arms against their Country, to become the executioners of their friends and Brethren, or to fall themselves by their Hands.

He has excited domestic insurrections amongst us, and has endeavoured to bring on the inhabitants of our frontiers, the merciless Indian Savages, whose known rule of warfare, is an undistinguished destruction of all ages, sexes and conditions.

In every stage of these Oppressions We have Petitioned for Redress in the most humble terms: Our repeated Petitions have been answered only by repeated injury. A Prince whose character is thus marked by every act which may define a Tyrant, is unfit to be the ruler of a free people.

Nor have We been wanting in attentions to our Brittish brethren. We have warned them from time to time of attempts by their legislature to extend an unwarrantable jurisdiction over us. We have reminded them of the circumstances of our emigration and settlement here. We have appealed to their native justice and magnanimity, and we have conjured them by the ties of our common kindred to disavow these usurpations, which, would inevitably interrupt our connections and correspondence. They too have been deaf to the voice of justice and of consanguinity. We must, therefore, acquiesce in the necessity, which denounces our Separation, and hold them, as we hold the rest of mankind, Enemies in War, in Peace Friends.

We, therefore, the Representatives of the united States of America, in General Congress, Assembled, appealing to the Supreme Judge of the world for the rectitude of our intentions, do, in the Name, and by Authority of the good People of these Colonies, solemnly publish and declare, That these United Colonies are, and of Right ought to be Free and Independent States; that they are Absolved from all Allegiance to the British Crown, and that all political connection between them and the State of Great Britain, is and ought to be totally dissolved; and that as Free and Independent States, they have full Power to levy War, conclude

Peace, contract Alliances, establish Commerce, and to do all other Acts and Things which Independent States may of right do. And for the support of this Declaration, with a firm reliance on the protection of divine Providence, we mutually pledge to each other our Lives, our Fortunes and our sacred Honor.

Georgia
Button Gwinnett
Lyman Hall
George Walton

North Carolina
William Hooper
Joseph Hewes
John Penn

South Carolina
Edward Rutledge
Thomas Heyward, Jr.
Thomas Lynch, Jr.
Arthur Middleton

Maryland
Samuel Chase
William Paca
Thomas Stone
Charles Carroll of Carrollton

Delaware
Caesar Rodney
George Read
Thomas McKean

Appendix E

The Constitution of the United States

(***This document was drafted primarily by James Madison and several others at the Constitutional Convention in Philadelphia in 1787. It was ratified in 1788, and put into effect in 1789.***)

Preamble

We the People of the United States, in Order to form a more perfect Union, establish Justice, insure domestic Tranquility, provide for the common defence, promote the general Welfare, and secure the Blessings of Liberty to ourselves and our Posterity, do ordain and establish this Constitution for the United States of America.

Article I - The Legislative Branch

Section 1 - The Legislature

All legislative Powers herein granted shall be vested in a Congress of the United States, which shall consist of a Senate and House of Representatives.

Section 2 - The House

The House of Representatives shall be composed of Members chosen every second Year by the People of the several States, and the Electors in each State shall have the Qualifications requisite for Electors of the most numerous Branch of the State Legislature.

No Person shall be a Representative who shall not have attained to the Age of twenty five Years, and been seven Years a Citizen of the United States, and who shall not, when elected, be an Inhabitant of that State in which he shall be chosen.

(*Representatives and direct Taxes shall be apportioned among the several States which may be included within this Union, according to their respective Numbers, which shall be determined by adding to the whole Number of free Persons, including those bound to Service for a Term of Years, and excluding Indians not taxed, three fifths of all other Persons.*) **(The previous sentence in parentheses was modified by the 14th Amendment, section 2.)** The actual Enumeration shall be made within three Years after the first Meeting of the Congress of the United States, and within every subsequent Term of ten Years, in such Manner as they shall by Law direct. The Number of Representatives shall exceed one for every thirty Thousand not, but each State shall have at Least one Representative; and until such enumeration shall be made, the State of New Hampshire shall be entitled to chuse three, Massachusetts eight, Rhode Island and Providence Plantations one, Connecticut five, New York six, New Jersey four, Pennsylvania eight, Delaware one, Maryland six, Virginia ten, North Carolina five, South Carolina five and Georgia three.

When vacancies happen in the Representation from any State, the Executive Authority thereof shall issue Writs of Election to fill such Vacancies.

The House of Representatives shall chuse their Speaker and other Officers; and shall have the sole Power of Impeachment.

Section 3 - The Senate

The Senate of the United States shall be composed of two Senators from each State, (*chosen by the Legislature thereof,*) **(The preceding words in parentheses superseded by 17th Amendment, section 1.)** for six Years; and each Senator shall have one Vote.

Immediately after they shall be assembled in Consequence of the first Election, they shall be divided as equally as may be into three Classes. The Seats of the Senators of the first Class shall be vacated at the Expiration of the second Year, of the second Class at the Expiration of the fourth Year, and of the third Class at the Expiration of the sixth Year, so that one third may be chosen every second Year; (*and if Vacancies happen by Resignation, or otherwise, during the Recess of the Legislature of any State, the Executive thereof may make temporary Appointments until the next Meeting of the Legislature, which shall then fill such Vacancies.*) **(The preceding words in parentheses were superseded by the 17th Amendment, section 2.)**

No person shall be a Senator who shall not have attained to the Age of thirty Years, and been nine Years a Citizen of the United States, and who shall not, when elected, be an Inhabitant of that State for which he shall be chosen.

The Vice President of the United States shall be President of the Senate, but shall have no Vote, unless they be equally divided.

The Senate shall chuse their other Officers, and also a President pro tempore, in the absence of the Vice President, or when he shall exercise the Office of President of the United States.

The Senate shall have the sole Power to try all Impeachments. When sitting for that Purpose, they shall be on Oath or Affirmation. When the President of the United States is tried, the Chief Justice shall preside: And no Person shall be convicted without the Concurrence of two thirds of the Members present.

Judgment in Cases of Impeachment shall not extend further than to removal from Office, and disqualification to hold and enjoy any Office of honor, Trust or Profit under the United States: but the Party convicted shall nevertheless be liable and subject to Indictment, Trial, Judgment and Punishment, according to Law.

Section 4 - Elections, Meetings

The Times, Places and Manner of holding Elections for Senators and Representatives, shall be prescribed in each State by the Legislature thereof; but the Congress may at any time by Law make or alter such Regulations, except as to the Place of Chusing Senators.

The Congress shall assemble at least once in every Year, and such Meeting shall (*be on the first Monday in December,*) (The preceding words in parentheses were superseded by the 20th Amendment, section 2.) unless they shall by Law appoint a different Day.

Section 5 - Membership, Rules, Journals, Adjourment

Each House shall be the Judge of the Elections, Returns and Qualifications of its own Members, and a Majority of each shall constitute a Quorum to do Business; but a smaller number may adjourn from day to day, and may be authorized to compel the Attendance of absent Members, in such Manner, and under such Penalties as each House may provide.

Each House may determine the Rules of its Proceedings, punish its Members for disorderly Behavior, and, with the Concurrence of two-thirds, expel a Member.

Each House shall keep a Journal of its Proceedings, and from time to time publish the same, excepting such Parts as may in their Judgment require Secrecy; and the Yeas and Nays of the Members of either House on any question shall, at the Desire of one fifth of those Present, be entered on the Journal.

Neither House, during the Session of Congress, shall, without the Consent of the other, adjourn for more than three days, nor to any other Place than that in which the two Houses shall be sitting.

Section 6 - Compensation

(*The Senators and Representatives shall receive a Compensation for their Services, to be ascertained by Law, and paid out of the Treasury of the United States.*) **(The preceding words in parentheses were modified by the 27th Amendment.)** They shall in all Cases, except Treason, Felony and Breach of the Peace, be privileged from Arrest during their Attendance at the Session of their respective Houses, and in going to and returning from the same; and for any Speech or Debate in either House, they shall not be questioned in any other Place.

No Senator or Representative shall, during the Time for which he was elected, be appointed to any civil Office under the Authority of the United States which shall have been created, or the Emoluments whereof shall have been increased during such time; and no Person holding any Office under the United States, shall be a Member of either House during his Continuance in Office.

Section 7 - Revenue Bills, Legislative Process, Presidential Veto

All bills for raising Revenue shall originate in the House of Representatives; but the Senate may propose or concur with Amendments as on other Bills.

Every Bill which shall have passed the House of Representatives and the Senate, shall, before it become a Law, be presented to the President of the United States; If he approve he shall sign it, but if not he shall return it, with his Objections to that House in which it shall have originated, who shall enter the Objections at large on their Journal, and proceed to reconsider it. If after such Reconsideration two thirds of that House shall agree to pass the Bill, it shall be sent, together with the Objections, to the other House, by which it shall likewise be reconsidered, and if approved by two thirds of that House, it shall become a Law. But in all such Cases the Votes of both Houses shall be determined by Yeas and Nays, and the Names of the Persons voting for and against the Bill shall be entered on the Journal of each House respectively. If any Bill shall not be returned by the President within ten Days (Sundays excepted) after it shall have been presented to him, the Same shall be a Law, in like Manner as if he had signed it, unless the Congress by their Adjournment prevent its Return, in which Case it shall not be a Law.

Every Order, Resolution, or Vote to which the Concurrence of the Senate and House of Representatives may be necessary (except on a question of Adjournment) shall be presented to the President of the United States; and before the Same shall take Effect, shall be approved by him, or being disapproved by him, shall be repassed by two thirds of the Senate and House of Representatives, according to the Rules and Limitations prescribed in the Case of a Bill.

Section 8 - Powers of Congress

The Congress shall have Power To lay and collect Taxes, Duties, Imposts and Excises, to pay the Debts and provide for the common Defence and general Welfare of the United States; but all Duties, Imposts and Excises shall be uniform throughout the United States;

To borrow money on the credit of the United States;

To regulate Commerce with foreign Nations, and among the several States, and with the Indian Tribes;

To establish an uniform Rule of Naturalization, and uniform Laws on the subject of Bankruptcies throughout the United States;

To coin Money, regulate the Value thereof, and of foreign Coin, and fix the Standard of Weights and Measures;

To provide for the Punishment of counterfeiting the Securities and current Coin of the United States;

To establish Post Offices and Post Roads;

To promote the Progress of Science and useful Arts, by securing for limited Times to Authors and Inventors the exclusive Right to their respective Writings and Discoveries;

To constitute Tribunals inferior to the supreme Court;

To define and punish Piracies and Felonies committed on the high Seas, and Offenses against the Law of Nations;

To declare War, grant Letters of Marque and Reprisal, and make Rules concerning Captures on Land and Water;

To raise and support Armies, but no Appropriation of Money to that Use shall be for a longer Term than two Years;

To provide and maintain a Navy;

To make Rules for the Government and Regulation of the land and naval Forces;

To provide for calling forth the Militia to execute the Laws of the Union, suppress Insurrections and repel Invasions;

To provide for organizing, arming, and disciplining, the Militia, and for governing such Part of them as may be employed in the Service of the United States, reserving to the States respectively, the Appointment of the Officers, and the Authority of training the Militia according to the discipline prescribed by Congress;

To exercise exclusive Legislation in all Cases whatsoever, over such District (not exceeding ten Miles square) as may, by Cession of particular States, and the acceptance of Congress, become the Seat of the Government of the United States, and to exercise like Authority over all Places purchased by the Consent of the Legislature of the State in which the Same shall be, for the Erection of Forts, Magazines, Arsenals, dock-Yards, and other needful Buildings; And

To make all Laws which shall be necessary and proper for carrying into Execution the foregoing Powers, and all other Powers vested by this Constitution in the Government of the United States, or in any Department or Officer thereof.

Section 9 - Limits on Congress

The Migration or Importation of such Persons as any of the States now existing shall think proper to admit, shall not be prohibited by the Congress prior to the Year one thousand eight hundred and eight, but a tax or duty may be imposed on such Importation, not exceeding ten dollars for each Person.

The privilege of the Writ of Habeas Corpus shall not be suspended, unless when in Cases of Rebellion or Invasion the public Safety may require it.

No Bill of Attainder or ex post facto Law shall be passed.

(*No capitation, or other direct, Tax shall be laid, unless in Proportion to the Census or Enumeration herein before directed to be taken.*) **(Section in parentheses clarified by the 16th Amendment.)**

No Tax or Duty shall be laid on Articles exported from any State.

No Preference shall be given by any Regulation of Commerce or Revenue to the Ports of one State over those of another: nor shall Vessels bound to, or from, one State, be obliged to enter, clear, or pay Duties in another.

No Money shall be drawn from the Treasury, but in Consequence of Appropriations made by Law; and a regular Statement and Account of the Receipts and Expenditures of all public Money shall be published from time to time.

No Title of Nobility shall be granted by the United States: And no Person holding any Office of Profit or Trust under them, shall, without the Consent of the Congress, accept of any present, Emolument, Office, or Title, of any kind whatever, from any King, Prince or foreign State.

Section 10 - Powers prohibited of States

No State shall enter into any Treaty, Alliance, or Confederation; grant Letters of Marque and Reprisal; coin Money; emit Bills of Credit; make any Thing but gold and silver Coin a Tender in Payment of Debts;

pass any Bill of Attainder, ex post facto Law, or Law impairing the Obligation of Contracts, or grant any Title of Nobility.

No State shall, without the Consent of the Congress, lay any Imposts or Duties on Imports or Exports, except what may be absolutely necessary for executing it's inspection Laws: and the net Produce of all Duties and Imposts, laid by any State on Imports or Exports, shall be for the Use of the Treasury of the United States; and all such Laws shall be subject to the Revision and Controul of the Congress.

No State shall, without the Consent of Congress, lay any duty of Tonnage, keep Troops, or Ships of War in time of Peace, enter into any Agreement or Compact with another State, or with a foreign Power, or engage in War, unless actually invaded, or in such imminent Danger as will not admit of delay.

Article II - The Executive Branch

Section 1 - The President

The executive Power shall be vested in a President of the United States of America. He shall hold his Office during the Term of four Years, and, together with the Vice-President chosen for the same Term, be elected, as follows:

Each State shall appoint, in such Manner as the Legislature thereof may direct, a Number of Electors, equal to the whole Number of Senators and Representatives to which the State may be entitled in the Congress: but no Senator or Representative, or Person holding an Office of Trust or Profit under the United States, shall be appointed an Elector.

(*The Electors shall meet in their respective States, and vote by Ballot for two persons, of whom one at least shall not lie an Inhabitant of the same State with themselves. And they shall make a List of all the Persons voted for, and of the Number of Votes for each; which List they shall sign and certify, and transmit sealed to the Seat of the Government of the United States, directed to the President of the Senate. The President of the Senate shall, in the Presence of the Senate and House of Representatives, open all the Certificates, and the Votes shall then be counted. The Person having the greatest Number of Votes shall be the President, if such Number be a Majority of the whole Number of Electors appointed; and if there be more than one who have such Majority, and have an equal Number of Votes, then the House of Representatives shall immediately chuse by Ballot one of them for President; and if no Person have a Majority, then from the five highest on the List the said House shall in like Manner chuse the President. But in chusing the President, the Votes shall be taken by States, the Representation from each State having one Vote; a quorum for this Purpose shall consist of a Member or Members from two-thirds of the States, and a Majority of all the States shall be necessary to a Choice. In every Case, after the Choice of the President, the Person having the greatest Number of Votes of the Electors shall be the Vice President. But if there should remain two or more who have equal Votes, the Senate shall chuse from them by Ballot the Vice-President.*) **(This clause in parentheses was superseded by the 12th Amendment.)**

The Congress may determine the Time of chusing the Electors, and the Day on which they shall give their Votes; which Day shall be the same throughout the United States.

No person except a natural born Citizen, or a Citizen of the United States, at the time of the Adoption of this Constitution, shall be eligible to the Office of President; neither shall any Person be eligible to that Office who shall not have attained to the Age of thirty-five Years, and been fourteen Years a Resident within the United States.

(*In Case of the Removal of the President from Office, or of his Death, Resignation, or Inability to discharge the Powers and Duties of the said Office, the same shall devolve on the Vice President, and the Congress may by Law provide for the Case of Removal, Death, Resignation or Inability, both of the President and Vice President, declaring what Officer shall then act as President, and such Officer shall act accordingly, until the Disability be removed, or a President shall be elected.*) **(This clause in parentheses has been modified by the 20th and 25th Amendments.)**

The President shall, at stated Times, receive for his Services, a Compensation, which shall neither be increased nor diminished during the Period for which he shall have been elected, and he shall not receive within that Period any other Emolument from the United States, or any of them.

Before he enter on the Execution of his Office, he shall take the following Oath or Affirmation:

"I do solemnly swear (or affirm) that I will faithfully execute the Office of President of the United States, and will to the best of my Ability, preserve, protect and defend the Constitution of the United States."

Section 2 - Civilian Power over Military, Cabinet, Pardon Power, Appointments

The President shall be Commander in Chief of the Army and Navy of the United States, and of the Militia of the several States, when called into the actual Service of the United States; he may require the Opinion, in writing, of the principal Officer in each of the executive Departments, upon any subject relating to the Duties of their respective Offices, and he shall have Power to Grant Reprieves and Pardons for Offenses against the United States, except in Cases of Impeachment.

He shall have Power, by and with the Advice and Consent of the Senate, to make Treaties, provided two thirds of the Senators present concur; and he shall nominate, and by and with the Advice and Consent of the Senate, shall appoint Ambassadors, other public Ministers and Consuls, Judges of the supreme Court, and all other Officers of the United States, whose Appointments are not herein otherwise provided for, and which shall be established by Law: but the Congress may by Law vest the Appointment of such inferior Officers, as they think proper, in the President alone, in the Courts of Law, or in the Heads of Departments.

The President shall have Power to fill up all Vacancies that may happen during the Recess of the Senate, by granting Commissions which shall expire at the End of their next Session.

Section 3 - State of the Union, Convening Congress

He shall from time to time give to the Congress Information of the State of the Union, and recommend to their Consideration such Measures as he shall judge necessary and expedient; he may, on extraordinary Occasions, convene both Houses, or either of them, and in Case of Disagreement between them, with Respect to the Time of Adjournment, he may adjourn them to such Time as he shall think proper; he shall receive Ambassadors and other public Ministers; he shall take Care that the Laws be faithfully executed, and shall Commission all the Officers of the United States.

Section 4 - Disqualification

The President, Vice President and all civil Officers of the United States, shall be removed from Office on Impeachment for, and Conviction of, Treason, Bribery, or other high Crimes and Misdemeanors.

Article III - The Judicial Branch

Section 1 - Judicial powers

The judicial Power of the United States, shall be vested in one supreme Court, and in such inferior Courts as the Congress may from time to time ordain and establish. The Judges, both of the supreme and inferior Courts, shall hold their Offices during good Behavior, and shall, at stated Times, receive for their Services a Compensation which shall not be diminished during their Continuance in Office.

Section 2 - Trial by Jury, Original Jurisdiction, Jury Trials

(*The judicial Power shall extend to all Cases, in Law and Equity, arising under this Constitution, the Laws of the United States, and Treaties made, or which shall be made, under their Authority; to all Cases affecting Ambassadors, other public Ministers and Consuls; to all Cases of admiralty and maritime Jurisdiction; to Controversies to which the United States shall be a Party; to Controversies between two or more States; between a State and Citizens of another State; between Citizens of different States; between Citizens of the same State claiming Lands under Grants of different States, and between a State, or the Citizens thereof, and foreign States, Citizens or Subjects.*) **(This section in parentheses is modified by the 11th Amendment.)**

In all Cases affecting Ambassadors, other public Ministers and Consuls, and those in which a State shall be Party, the supreme Court shall have original Jurisdiction. In all the other Cases before mentioned, the supreme Court shall have appellate Jurisdiction, both as to Law and Fact, with such Exceptions, and under such Regulations as the Congress shall make.

The Trial of all Crimes, except in Cases of Impeachment, shall be by Jury; and such Trial shall be held in the State where the said Crimes shall have been committed; but when not committed within any State, the Trial shall be at such Place or Places as the Congress may by Law have directed.

Section 3 – Treason

Treason against the United States, shall consist only in levying War against them, or in adhering to their Enemies, giving them Aid and Comfort. No Person shall be convicted of Treason unless on the Testimony of two Witnesses to the same overt Act, or on Confession in open Court.

The Congress shall have power to declare the Punishment of Treason, but no Attainder of Treason shall work Corruption of Blood, or Forfeiture except during the Life of the Person attainted.

Article IV - The States

Section 1 - Each State to Honor all others

Full Faith and Credit shall be given in each State to the public Acts, Records, and judicial Proceedings of every other State. And the Congress may by general Laws prescribe the Manner in which such Acts, Records and Proceedings shall be proved, and the Effect thereof.

Section 2 - State citizens, Extradition

The Citizens of each State shall be entitled to all Privileges and Immunities of Citizens in the several States.

A Person charged in any State with Treason, Felony, or other Crime, who shall flee from Justice, and be found in another State, shall on demand of the executive Authority of the State from which he fled, be delivered up, to be removed to the State having Jurisdiction of the Crime.

(No Person held to Service or Labour in one State, under the Laws thereof, escaping into another, shall, in Consequence of any Law

or Regulation therein, be discharged from such Service or Labour, But shall be delivered up on Claim of the Party to whom such Service or Labour may be due.) **(This clause in parentheses is superseded by the 13th Amendment.)**

Section 3 - New States

New States may be admitted by the Congress into this Union; but no new States shall be formed or erected within the Jurisdiction of any other State; nor any State be formed by the Junction of two or more States, or parts of States, without the Consent of the Legislatures of the States concerned as well as of the Congress.

The Congress shall have Power to dispose of and make all needful Rules and Regulations respecting the Territory or other Property belonging to the United States; and nothing in this Constitution shall be so construed as to Prejudice any Claims of the United States, or of any particular State.

Section 4 - Republican government

The United States shall guarantee to every State in this Union a Republican Form of Government, and shall protect each of them against Invasion; and on Application of the Legislature, or of the Executive (when the Legislature cannot be convened) against domestic Violence.

Article V - Amendment

The Congress, whenever two thirds of both Houses shall deem it necessary, shall propose Amendments to this Constitution, or, on the Application of the Legislatures of two thirds of the several States, shall call a Convention for proposing Amendments, which, in either Case, shall be valid to all Intents and Purposes, as part of this Constitution, when ratified by the Legislatures of three fourths of the several States, or by Conventions in three fourths thereof, as the one or the other Mode of Ratification may be proposed by the Congress; Provided that no Amendment which may be made prior to the Year One thousand eight hundred and eight shall in any Manner affect the first and fourth Clauses in the Ninth Section of the first Article; and that no State, without its Consent, shall be deprived of its equal Suffrage in the Senate.

Article VI - Debts, Supremacy, Oaths

All Debts contracted and Engagements entered into, before the Adoption of this Constitution, shall be as valid against the United States under this Constitution, as under the Confederation.

This Constitution, and the Laws of the United States which shall be made in Pursuance thereof; and all Treaties made, or which shall be made, under the Authority of the United States, shall be the supreme Law of the Land; and the Judges in every State shall be bound thereby, any Thing in the Constitution or Laws of any State to the Contrary notwithstanding.

The Senators and Representatives before mentioned, and the Members of the several State Legislatures, and all executive and judicial Officers, both of the United States and of the several States, shall be bound by Oath or Affirmation, to support this Constitution; but no religious Test shall ever be required as a Qualification to any Office or public Trust under the United States.

Article VII - Ratification

The Ratification of the Conventions of nine States, shall be sufficient for the Establishment of this Constitution between the States so ratifying the Same.

The Word, "the," being interlined between the seventh and eighth Lines of the first Page, the Word "Thirty" being partly written on an Erazure in the fifteenth Line of the first Page, The Words "is tried" being interlined between the thirty second and thirty third Lines of the first Page and the Word "the" being interlined between the forty third and forty fourth Lines of the second Page.

Attest William Jackson Secretary

Done in Convention by the Unanimous Consent of the States present the Seventeenth Day of September in the Year of our Lord one thousand seven hundred and Eighty seven and of the Independence of the United States of America the Twelfth In witness whereof We have hereunto subscribed our Names.

G. Washington
Presidt and deputy from Virginia

Delaware	**Maryland**	**Virginia**
Geo: Read	James McHenry	John Blair
Gunning Bedford jun	Dan of St Thos. Jenifer	James Madison
John Dickinson	Danl. Carroll	
Richard Bassett		
Jaco: Broom		
North Carolina	**South Carolina**	**Georgia**
Wm. Blount	J. Rutledge	William Few
Richd. Dobbs Spaight	Charles Cotesworth Pinckney	Abr Baldwin
Hu Williamson	Charles Pinckney	
	Pierce Butler	
New Hampshire	**Massachusetts**	**Connecticut**
John Langdon	Nathaniel Gorham	Wm. Saml. Johnson
Nicholas Gilman	Rufus King	Roger Sherman
New York	**New Jersey**	**Pennsylvania**
Alexander Hamilton	Wil: Livingston	B. Franklin
	David Brearly	Thomas Mifflin
	Wm. Patterson	Robt. Morris
	Jona: Dayton	Geo. Clymer
	Jona: Dayton	Thos. FitzSimons
		Jared Ingersoll
		James Wilson
		Gouv Morris

Appendix F

The Amendments to the Constitution

(The first 10 Amendments to the Constitution of the United States are known as the Bill of Rights. These Amendments were passed by the first Congress under the Constitution, and were ratified December 15, 1791. The other Amendments were passed by other Congresses over the years and ratified.)

Amendment I

Congress shall make no law respecting an establishment of religion, or prohibiting the free exercise thereof; or abridging the freedom of speech, or of the press; or the right of the people peaceably to assemble, and to petition the Government for a redress of grievances.

Amendment II

A well regulated Militia, being necessary to the security of a free State, the right of the people to keep and bear Arms, shall not be infringed.

Amendment III

No Soldier shall, in time of peace be quartered in any house, without the consent of the Owner, nor in time of war, but in a manner to be prescribed by law.

Amendment IV

The right of the people to be secure in their persons, houses, papers, and effects, against unreasonable searches and seizures, shall not be violated, and no Warrants shall issue, but upon probable cause, supported by Oath or affirmation, and particularly describing the place to be searched, and the persons or things to be seized.

Amendment V

No person shall be held to answer for a capital, or otherwise infamous crime, unless on a presentment or indictment of a Grand Jury, except in cases arising in the land or naval forces, or in the Militia, when in actual service in time of War or public danger; nor shall any person be subject for the same offense to be twice put in jeopardy of life or limb; nor shall be compelled in any criminal case to be a witness against himself, nor be deprived of life, liberty, or property, without due process of law; nor shall private property be taken for public use, without just compensation.

Amendment VI

In all criminal prosecutions, the accused shall enjoy the right to a speedy and public trial, by an impartial jury of the State and district wherein the crime shall have been committed, which district shall have been previously ascertained by law, and to be informed of the nature and cause of the accusation; to be confronted with the witnesses against him; to have compulsory process for obtaining witnesses in his favor, and to have the Assistance of Counsel for his defence.

Amendment VII

In Suits at common law, where the value in controversy shall exceed twenty dollars, the right of trial by jury shall be preserved, and no fact tried by a jury, shall be otherwise re-examined in any Court of the United States, than according to the rules of the common law.

Amendment VIII

Excessive bail shall not be required, nor excessive fines imposed, nor cruel and unusual punishments inflicted.

Amendment IX

The enumeration in the Constitution, of certain rights, shall not be construed to deny or disparage others retained by the people.

Amendment X

The powers not delegated to the United States by the Constitution, nor prohibited by it to the States, are reserved to the States respectively, or to the people.

Amendment XI

(*This Amendment was passed by Congress March 4, 1794, and was ratified February 7, 1795. Note: Article III, section 2 of the Constitution was modified by this Amendment.*)

The Judicial power of the United States shall not be construed to extend to any suit in law or equity, commenced or prosecuted against one of the United States by Citizens of another State, or by Citizens or Subjects of any Foreign State.

Amendment XII

(***This Amendment was passed by Congress December 9, 1803, and was ratified June 15, 1804. Note: Part of Article II, section 1 of the Constitution was superseded by this Amendment.***)

The Electors shall meet in their respective states, and vote by ballot for President and Vice-President, one of whom, at least, shall not be an inhabitant of the same state with themselves; they shall name in their ballots the person voted for as President, and in distinct ballots the person voted for as Vice-President, and they shall make distinct lists of all persons voted for as President, and of all persons voted for as Vice-President and of the number of votes for each, which lists they shall sign and certify, and transmit sealed to the seat of the government of the United States, directed to the President of the Senate;

The President of the Senate shall, in the presence of the Senate and House of Representatives, open all the certificates and the votes shall then be counted;

The person having the greatest Number of votes for President, shall be the President, if such number be a majority of the whole number of Electors appointed; and if no person have such majority, then from the persons having the highest numbers not exceeding three on the list of those voted for as President, the House of Representatives shall choose immediately, by ballot, the President. But in choosing the President, the votes shall be taken by states, the representation from each state having one vote; a quorum for this purpose shall consist of a member or members from two-thirds of the states, and a majority of all the states shall be necessary to a choice. And if the House of Representatives shall not choose a President whenever the right of choice shall devolve upon them, before the fourth day of March next following, then the Vice-President shall act as President, as in the case of the death or other constitutional disability of the President.*

The person having the greatest number of votes as Vice-President, shall be the Vice-President, if such number be a majority of the whole number of Electors appointed, and if no person have a majority, then from the two highest numbers on the list, the Senate shall choose the Vice-President; a quorum for the purpose shall consist of two-thirds of the whole number of Senators, and a majority of the whole number shall be necessary to a choice. But no person constitutionally ineligible to the office of President shall be eligible to that of Vice-President of the United States.

****Superseded by section 3 of Amendment XX.***

Amendment XIII

(***This Amendment was passed by Congress January 31, 1865, and was ratified December 6, 1865. Note: a part of Article IV, section 2 of the Constitution was superseded by this Amendment.***)

Section 1. Neither slavery nor involuntary servitude, except as a punishment for crime whereof the party shall have been duly convicted, shall exist within the United States, or any place subject to their jurisdiction.

Section 2. Congress shall have power to enforce this article by appropriate legislation.

Amendment XIV

(***This Amendment was passed by Congress June 13, 1866, and was ratified July 9, 1868. Note: Article I, section 2, of the Constitution was modified by section 2 of this Amendment.***)

Section 1. All persons born or naturalized in the United States, and subject to the jurisdiction thereof, are citizens of the United States and of the State wherein they reside. No State shall make or enforce any law which shall abridge the privileges or immunities of citizens of the United States; nor shall any State deprive any person of life, liberty, or property, without due process of law; nor deny to any person within its jurisdiction the equal protection of the laws.

Section 2. Representatives shall be apportioned among the several States according to their respective numbers, counting the whole number of persons in each State, excluding Indians not taxed. But when the right to vote at any election for the choice of electors for President and Vice-President of the United States, Representatives in Congress, the Executive and Judicial officers of a State, or the members of the Legislature thereof, is denied to any of the male inhabitants of such State, being twenty-one years of age,* and citizens of the United States, or in any way abridged, except for participation in rebellion, or other crime, the basis of representation therein shall be reduced in the proportion which the number of such male citizens shall bear to the whole number of male citizens twenty-one years of age in such State.

Section 3. No person shall be a Senator or Representative in Congress, or elector of President and Vice-President, or hold any office, civil or military, under the United States, or under any State, who, having previously taken an oath, as a member of Congress, or as an officer of the United States, or as a member of any State legislature, or as an executive or judicial officer of any State, to support the Constitution of the United States, shall have engaged in insurrection or rebellion against the same, or given aid or comfort to the enemies thereof. But Congress may by a vote of two-thirds of each House, remove such disability.

Section 4. The validity of the public debt of the United States, authorized by law, including debts incurred for payment of pensions and bounties for services in suppressing insurrection or rebellion, shall not be questioned. But neither the United States nor any State shall assume or pay any debt or obligation incurred in aid of insurrection or rebellion against the United States, or any claim for the loss or emancipation of any slave; but all such debts, obligations and claims shall be held illegal and void.

Section 5. The Congress shall have power to enforce, by appropriate legislation, the provisions of this article.

Changed by section 1 of Amendment XXVI.

Amendment XV

(***This Amendment was passed by Congress February 26, 1869, and was ratified February 3, 1870.***)

Section 1. The right of citizens of the United States to vote shall not be denied or abridged by the United States or by any State on account of race, color, or previous condition of servitude.

Section 2. The Congress shall have power to enforce this article by appropriate legislation.

Amendment XVI

(***This Amendment was passed by Congress July 2, 1909, and was ratified February 3, 1913. Note: Article I, section 9, of the Constitution was modified by this Amendment.***)

The Congress shall have power to lay and collect taxes on incomes, from whatever source derived, without apportionment among the several States, and without regard to any census or enumeration.

Amendment XVII

(***This Amendment was passed by Congress May 13, 1912, and was ratified April 8, 1913. Note: Article I, section 3, of the Constitution was modified by this Amendment.***)

The Senate of the United States shall be composed of two Senators from each State, elected by the people thereof, for six years; and each Senator shall have one vote. The electors in each State shall have the qualifications requisite for electors of the most numerous branch of the State legislatures.

When vacancies happen in the representation of any State in the Senate, the executive authority of such State shall issue writs of election to fill such vacancies: Provided, That the legislature of any State may empower the executive thereof to make temporary appointments until the people fill the vacancies by election as the legislature may direct.

This amendment shall not be so construed as to affect the election or term of any Senator chosen before it becomes valid as part of the Constitution.

Amendment XVIII

(***This Amendment was passed by Congress December 18, 1917, and was ratified January 16, 1919. It was repealed by Amendment XXI.***)

Section 1. After one year from the ratification of this article the manufacture, sale, or transportation of intoxicating liquors within, the importation thereof into, or the exportation thereof from the United States and all territory subject to the jurisdiction thereof for beverage purposes is hereby prohibited.

Section 2. The Congress and the several States shall have concurrent power to enforce this article by appropriate legislation.

Section 3. This article shall be inoperative unless it shall have been ratified as an amendment to the Constitution by the legislatures of the several States, as provided in the Constitution, within seven years from the date of the submission hereof to the States by the Congress.

Amendment XIX

(***This Amendment was passed by Congress June 4, 1919, and was ratified August 18, 1920.***)

The right of citizens of the United States to vote shall not be denied or abridged by the United States or by any State on account of sex.

Congress shall have power to enforce this article by appropriate legislation.

Amendment XX

(***This Amendment was passed by Congress March 2, 1932, and was ratified January 23, 1933. Note: Article I, section 4, of the Constitution was modified by section 2 of this Amendment. In addition, a part of Amendment XII was superseded by section 3.***)

Section 1. The terms of the President and Vice President shall end at noon on the 20th day of January, and the terms of Senators and Representatives at noon on the 3d day of January, of the years in which such terms would have ended if this article had not been ratified; and the terms of their successors shall then begin.

Section 2. The Congress shall assemble at least once in every year, and such meeting shall begin at noon on the 3d day of January, unless they shall by law appoint a different day.

Section 3. If, at the time fixed for the beginning of the term of the President, the President elect shall have died, the Vice President elect shall become President. If a President shall not have been chosen before the time fixed for the beginning of his term, or if the President elect shall have failed to qualify, then the Vice President elect shall act as President until a President shall have qualified; and the Congress may by law provide for the case wherein neither a President elect nor a Vice President elect shall have qualified, declaring who shall then act as

President, or the manner in which one who is to act shall be selected, and such person shall act accordingly until a President or Vice President shall have qualified.

Section 4. The Congress may by law provide for the case of the death of any of the persons from whom the House of Representatives may choose a President whenever the right of choice shall have devolved upon them, and for the case of the death of any of the persons from whom the Senate may choose a Vice President whenever the right of choice shall have devolved upon them.

Section 5. Sections 1 and 2 shall take effect on the 15th day of October following the ratification of this article.

Section 6. This article shall be inoperative unless it shall have been ratified as an amendment to the Constitution by the legislatures of three-fourths of the several States within seven years from the date of its submission.

Amendment XXI

(***This Amendment was passed by Congress February 20, 1933, and was ratified December 5, 1933.***)

Section 1. The eighteenth article of amendment to the Constitution of the United States is hereby repealed.

Section 2. The transportation or importation into any State, Territory, or possession of the United States for delivery or use therein of intoxicating liquors, in violation of the laws thereof, is hereby prohibited.

Section 3. The article shall be inoperative unless it shall have been ratified as an amendment to the Constitution by conventions in the several States, as provided in the Constitution, within seven years from the date of the submission hereof to the States by the Congress.

Amendment XXII

(***This Amendment was passed by Congress March 21, 1947, and was ratified February 17, 1951.***)

Section 1. No person shall be elected to the office of the President more than twice, and no person who has held the office of President, or acted as President, for more than two years of a term to which some other person was elected President shall be elected to the office of the President more than once. But this Article shall not apply to any person holding the office of President, when this Article was proposed by the Congress, and shall not prevent any person who may be holding the office of President, or acting as President, during the term within which this Article becomes operative from holding the office of President or acting as President during the remainder of such term.

Section 2. This article shall be inoperative unless it shall have been ratified as an amendment to the Constitution by the legislatures of three-fourths of the several States within seven years from the date of its submission to the States by the Congress.

Amendment XXIII

(***This Amendment was passed by Congress June 16, 1960, and was ratified March 29, 1961.***)

Section 1. The District constituting the seat of Government of the United States shall appoint in such manner as the Congress may direct: A number of electors of President and Vice President equal to the whole number of Senators and Representatives in Congress to which the District would be entitled if it were a State, but in no event more than the least populous State; they shall be in addition to those appointed by the States, but they shall be considered, for the purposes of the election of President and Vice President, to be electors appointed by a State; and they shall meet in the District and perform such duties as provided by the twelfth article of amendment.

Section 2. The Congress shall have power to enforce this article by appropriate legislation.

Amendment XXIV

(***This Amendment was passed by Congress August 27, 1962, and was ratified January 23, 1964.***)

Section 1. The right of citizens of the United States to vote in any primary or other election for President or Vice President, for electors for President or Vice President, or for Senator or Representative in Congress, shall not be denied or abridged by the United States or any State by reason of failure to pay any poll tax or other tax.

Section 2. The Congress shall have power to enforce this article by appropriate legislation.

Amendment XXV

(***This Amendment was passed by Congress July 6, 1965, and was ratified February 10, 1967. Note: Article II, section 1, of the Constitution was affected by this Amendment.***)

Section 1. In case of the removal of the President from office or of his death or resignation, the Vice President shall become President.

Section 2. Whenever there is a vacancy in the office of the Vice President, the President shall nominate a Vice President who shall take office upon confirmation by a majority vote of both Houses of Congress.

Section 3. Whenever the President transmits to the President pro tempore of the Senate and the Speaker of the House of Representatives his written declaration that he is unable to discharge the powers and duties of his office, and until he transmits to them a written declaration to the contrary, such powers and duties shall be discharged by the Vice President as Acting President.

Section 4. Whenever the Vice President and a majority of either the principal officers of the executive departments or of such other body as Congress may by law provide, transmit to the President pro tempore of the Senate and the Speaker of the House of Representatives their written declaration that the President is unable to discharge the powers and duties of his office, the Vice President shall immediately assume the powers and duties of the office as Acting President.

Thereafter, when the President transmits to the President pro tempore of the Senate and the Speaker of the House of Representatives his written declaration that no inability exists, he shall resume the powers and duties of his office unless the Vice President and a majority of either the principal officers of the executive department or of such other body as Congress may by law provide, transmit within four days to the President pro tempore of the Senate and the Speaker of the House of Representatives their written declaration that the President is unable to discharge the powers and duties of his office. Thereupon Congress shall decide the issue, assembling within forty eight hours for that purpose if not in session. If the Congress, within twenty one days after receipt of the latter written declaration, or, if Congress is not in session, within twenty one days after Congress is required to assemble, determines by two thirds vote of both Houses that the President is unable to discharge the powers and duties of his office, the Vice President shall continue to discharge the same as Acting President; otherwise, the President shall resume the powers and duties of his office.

Amendment XXVI

(***This Amendment was passed by Congress March 23, 1971, and was ratified July 1, 1971. Note: Amendment XIV, section 2, of the Constitution was modified by section 1 of this Amendment.***)

Section 1. The right of citizens of the United States, who are eighteen years of age or older, to vote shall not be denied or abridged by the United States or by any State on account of age.

Section 2. The Congress shall have power to enforce this article by appropriate legislation.

Amendment XXVII

(***This Amendment was proposed September 25, 1789. It was ratified May 7, 1992.***)

No law, varying the compensation for the services of the Senators and Representatives, shall take effect, until an election of Representatives shall have intervened.

Bibliography*

Ahlstrom, Sydney E. *A Religious History of the American People*. New Haven: Yale University Press, 1972.

Applegate, Edd. *Advocacy Journalists: A Biographical Dictionary of Writers and Editors*. Lanham, Maryland: The Scarecrow Press, Inc., 2009.

Applegate, Edd. *Muckrakers: A Biographical Dictionary of Writers and Editors*. Lanham, Maryland: The Scarecrow Press, Inc., 2008.

Blum, John. *Years of Discord in Politics and Society, 1961-74*. New York: W. W. Norton, 1991.

Brasch, Walter M. *Forerunners of Revolution: Muckrakers and the American Social Conscience*. Lanham, MD: University Press of America, 1990.

Brendon, Piers. *The Life and Death of the Press Barons*. New York: Atheneum, 1983.

Brown, Dee. *Bury My Heart at Wounded Knee: An American Indian History of the American West*. New York: Holt, Rinehart and Winston, 1970.

Carter, Paul A. *The Spiritual Crisis of the Gilded Age*. DeKalb: Northern Illinois University Press, 1971.

Chadwick, French E. *Relations of the United States and Spain: the Spanish-American War* (2 vols). New York: Russell & Russell, 1968.

Chalmers, David Mark. *The Social and Political Ideas of the Muckrakers*. New York: Citadel, 1964.

Channing, Edward. *History of the United States* (6 vols.). New York: Macmillan, 1905-25.

Collier, John. *Indians of the Americas*. New York: New American Library, 1963.

Curti, Merle. *The Growth of American Thought* (3rd ed.). New York: Harper & Row, 1964.

Curti, Merle. *A History of American Civilization*. New York: Harper & Row, 1953.

Dewey, Davis R. *Financial History of the United States* (12th ed.). New York: A. M. Kelley, 1968.

Diamond, Jared. *Guns, Germs and Steel: The Fates of Human Societies*. New York: W.W. Norton, 1998.

Dray, Philip. *At the Hands of Persons Unknown: The Lynching of Black America*. New York: Random House, 2002.

Drewry, John E., ed. *Post Biographies of Famous Journalists*. Athens: University of Georgia Press, 1942.

Ely, Richard T. *The Labor Movement in America*. New York: Arno Press, 1969.

Faulkner, Harold U. *American Economic History* (8th ed.). New York: Harper & Row, 1966.

Ferguson, Niall. *The Pity of War*. New York: Basic Books, 1999.

Filler, Louis. *The Muckrakers*. University Park: Pennsylvania State University Press, 1976.

FitzGerald, Frances. *Fire in the Lake: the Vietnamese and the Americans in Vietnam*. Boston: Atlantic-Little, Brown, 1972.

Foner, Philip. *A History of the Labor Movement in the United States* (4 vols.). New York: International Publishers, 1947-1964.

Friedman, Lawrence M. *Crime and Punishment in American History*. New York: Basic Books, 1993.

Garrow, David J. *Bearing the Cross: Martin Luther King, Jr., and the Southern Christian Leadership Conference*. New York: Morrow, 1986.

Goodwyn, Lawrence. *Democratic Promise: The Populist Movement in America*. New York: Oxford University Press, 1976.

Graham, Otis L., Jr. *An Encore for Reform: The Old Progressives and the New Deal*. New York: Oxford University Press, 1967.

Halberstam, David. *The Best and the Brightest*. New York: Random House, 1972.

Halberstam, David. *War in a Time of Peace: Bush, Clinton, and the Generals*. New York: Scribner's Sons, 2001.

Heilbroner, Robert and Aaron Singer. *The Economic Transformation of America*. New York: Harcourt Brace Jovanovich, 1977.

Hill, Frances. *A Delusion of Satan: The Full Story of the Salem Witch Trials*. New York: Da Capo Press, 1997.

Hofstadter, Richard. *The Age of Reform: From Bryan to F.D.R.* New York: Knopf, 1955.

Hudson, Frederic. *Journalism in the United States, from 1690-1872*. New York: Harper, 1873.

Hughes, Jonathan. *The Vital Few: American Economic Progress and Its Protagonists*. New York: Oxford University Press, 1986.

Jarrett, Greg. *The Russia Hoax: The Illicit Scheme to Clear Hillary Clinton and Frame Donald Trump*. New York: Broadside Books, 2018.

Josephson, Matthew. *The Robber Barons: The Great American Capitalists, 1861-1901*. New York: Harcourt, Brace, 1934.

Karnow, Stanley. *Vietnam: A History*. New York: Viking Penguin, 1983.

Kennedy, Paul. *The Rise and Fall of the Great Powers: Economic Change and Military Conflict from 1500 to 2000*. New York: Random House, 1987.

Knott, Stephen F. *Secret and Sanctioned: Covert Operations and the American Presidency*. Oxford: Oxford University Press, 1996.

Knox, Dudley W. *A History of the United States Navy* (rev. ed.). New York: G. P. Putnam's Sons, 1938.

Kolko, Gabriel. *The Triumph of Conservatism*. New York: Free Press, 1977.

Lukas, J. Anthony. *Nightmare: The Underside of the Nixon Years*. New York: Viking, 1976.

McMaster, John B. *A History of the People of the United States from the Revolution to the Civil War* (6 vols.). New York: D. Appleton and Co., 1895.

Meinig, D. W. *The Shaping of America: Continental America, 1800-1967*. New Haven: Yale University Press, 1993.

Morison, Samuel Eliot and Henry Steele Commager. *The Growth of the American Republic* (2 vols.). New York: Oxford University Press, 1962.

Mott, Frank Luther. *American Journalism: A History, 1690-1960*. New York: Macmillan, 1962.

Neely, Richard. *How Courts Govern America*. New Haven: Yale University Press, 1981.

Phillips, Kevin. *Wealth and Democracy: A Political History of the American Rich*. New York: Broadway Books, 2002.

Potter, D. M. *People of Plenty: Economic Abundance and the American Character*. Chicago: University of Chicago Press, 1954.

Prucha, Francis P. *The Great Father: the United States Government and the American Indians* (2 vols.). Lincoln: University of Nebraska Press, 1984.

Regier, C. C. *The Era of the Muckrakers*. Chapel Hill: University of North Carolina Press, 1932.

Schweizer, Peter. *Profiles in Corruption: Abuse of Power by America's Progressive Elite*. New York: Harper, 2020.

Smith, Lee. *The Permanent Coup: How Enemies Foreign and Domestic Targeted the American President*. New York: Center Street, 2020.

Sorenson, Thomas C. *The Word War. The Story of American Propaganda*. New York: Harper & Row, 1968.

Steinberg, Stephen. *The Ethnic Myth: Race, Ethnicity and Class in America*. New York: Atheneum, 1981.

Tanssig, F. W. *The Tariff History of the United States: A Series of Essays*. New York: G. P. Putnam's Sons, 1923.

Taylor, A. J. P. *The War Lords*. New York: Penguin Press, 1976.

Weinberg, Albert K. *Manifest Destiny: A Study of Nationalist Expansion in American History*. Baltimore: The Johns Hopkins Press, 1935.

White, Donald W. *The American Century: the Rise and Decline of the United States as a World Power*. New Haven: Yale University Press, 1996.

White, Theodore. *America in Search of Itself: The Making of the President, 1956-1980*. New York: Harper & Row, 1982.

Williams, T. Harry. *The History of American Wars: From 1745 to 1918*. New York: Knopf, 1985.

---

*In addition to the references listed at the end of each chapter, the books listed above were helpful.

About the Author

Edd Applegate, Professor Emeritus, taught undergraduate and graduate courses at several colleges and universities for more than 30 years. Prior to teaching he worked in public relations for a state educational organization, for which he wrote numerous articles that were published in various newspapers.

He has written several books, including *The Rise of Advertising in the United States: A History of Innovation to 1960*, *Journalism in the United States: Concepts and Issues*, *The Advocacy Journalists: A Biographical Dictionary of Writers and Editors*, and *Muckrakers: A Biographical Dictionary of Writers and Editors*, to mention a few.

He has contributed numerous chapters and entries to other nonfiction books and encyclopedias. His scholarly research and reviews of books have been published in *American Journalism*, *ASJMC INSIGHTS, CHOICE, Feedback, JACA: Journal of the Association for Communication Administration, Journal of Advertising Education, Journalism and Mass Communication Educator, Journalism and Mass Communication Quarterly, Journalism History, Journalism Studies,* and *Public Relations Quarterly*, among other academic journals. Other scholarly research has been presented at international and national academic conferences and published in various proceedings.

Applegate has received grants and fellowships from the Freedom Forum Media Studies Center, the Gannett Foundation, the Missouri Commission on Humanities, the National Endowment for the Humanities, the American Association of Advertising Agencies, the American Press Institute, the Donald and Geraldine Hedberg Foundation, the Direct Marketing Educational Foundation, and other organizations.

He received his doctorate from Oklahoma State University. He continued his formal education at Pennsylvania State University and

Vanderbilt University, among other universities, before he retired from teaching.

Index

T

www.ingramcontent.com/pod-product-compliance
Lightning Source LLC
LaVergne TN
LVHW010718210926
848485LV00008B/1445/J